# Coping with
# Natural Disasters

# Coping with Natural Disasters

## CAROLINE ARNOLD

WALKER AND COMPANY    NEW YORK

First published in the United States of America in 1988 by the Walker
Publishing Company, Inc. Published simultaneously in Canada
by Thomas Allen & Son.
Canada, Limited, Markham, Ontario

Designed by Angela Foote

Library of Congress Cataloging-in-Publication Data

Arnold, Caroline.
  Coping with natural disasters.

  Bibliography: p.
  Includes index.
  1. Natural disasters.   2.  Disaster relief.
I.  Title.
GB5014.A76  1987          363.3′4          87-37279
ISBN 0-8027-6716-8
ISBN 0-8027-6717-6 (lib. bdg.)

Printed in the United States of America

10 9 8 7 6 5 4 3 2 1

# Author's Note

Although disaster relief personnel freely offer help to all in need and do not distinguish between victims of natural disasters and man-made calamities such as transportation accidents, collapsed bridges, or industrial explosions, this book is limited to the discussion of sudden, natural disasters. These disasters come either without warning or with little time to escape. Droughts have not been included because they are not sudden calamities, even though they often have disastrous consequences for the people affected. It is hoped that this book will stimulate discussions both at home and in school regarding preparing for and dealing with emergencies.

Each part of the world is prone to certain types of natural disasters. For instance, hurricanes are the biggest threat to certain coastal areas, whereas, tornadoes are the primary danger in many inland parts of the United States. Communities along rivers need to be aware of possible floods. People who live in the western United States and other parts of the world located along fault lines need to know about earthquakes. Even if a particular disaster is not likely to occur where you live, knowing about how it affects people will help you to better understand news reports about local and international disasters.

Disasters caused by violent movements of the earth, large fires, and unusual weather conditions are natural events that have been occurring for millions of years. They are awesome and often frightening, but as we learn more about them we can be better prepared to cope with them in the future.

I am grateful for all the help I received on this project from the Los Angeles Chapter of the American Red Cross, which provided photographs and information, and from Dr. Alfred Zerfas, a medical epidemiologist, who has worked in emergency situations in Nigeria, India, Bangladesh, and Somalia, for providing research materials and expert advice. For assistance in obtaining photographs I thank the United States Department of the Interior; Mrs. J. C. David of the National Oceanic and Atmospheric Administration; Clyde McNair, United States Agency for International Development; Robert Brady of the United States Department of Agriculture Forest Service; and Lester Scheaffer. I also thank Elizabeth Fisher and Robert Hadley for their translation of Pliny the Younger's letter describing the eruption of Mount Vesuvius in Italy in 79 A.D.

*Caroline Arnold*
*Los Angeles, California*

# Contents

# Coping with
# Natural Disasters

# CHAPTER ONE

# People Who Help: The Work of Relief Organizations

At 7:18 in the morning, on September 19, 1985, residents of Mexico City felt the earth beneath them tremble. Trees swayed violently and buildings shuddered, their walls and supports groaning from the stress. Along the street, telephone and electrical lines snapped, metal lampposts swayed and bent, and underground gas lines broke and burst into flames. For a long, terrifying minute the whole world seemed to be in motion, and when it stopped, windows were broken, walls were cracked, and hundreds of buildings had collapsed into heaps of concrete and steel.

The initial *tremor*, lasting less than a minute, was followed by at least twenty smaller tremors called *aftershocks*, which destroyed about 250 buildings. The Mexican armed forces reported that about 400 people had died, but as people combed the wreckage in search of victims, the death toll rose rapidly to over 2,000 and appeared as if it would climb even higher. Then, on the evening of September 21, a second large tremor shook the city once again. Terrified citizens fled into the streets and several dozen buildings, already damaged by the first earthquake, crumbled completely. So many people were buried that it was impossible to know exactly how many had died. The American Ambassador to Mexico reported in a news conference that it was likely that at least 7,200 people were dead, most of them killed by falling concrete or crushed in piles of rubble. Thousands more were trapped or injured, many of whom died because they were reached too late.

Almost immediately after the first tremor, word went out across the world that a terrible earthquake had struck in Mexico City. Specific details were slow to reach the outside world because the main transmitter for long-distance telephone calls was destroyed when the main broadcast tower collapsed. Amateur short-wave radio operators were one of the only groups able to convey information outside the city for the first few days.

Mexican armed forces and local police were the first relief groups to respond to the disaster. About thirty army helicopters hovered over damaged areas while about 600 policemen joined Army and Navy personnel in closing off the most dangerous city blocks. With the help of thousands of civilian volunteers, they began to pull bodies out of the wreckage. There were so many victims that the dead were simply left on the street with the word *muerto* (Spanish for dead), written in chalk on the pavement, so that the wounded could be given first aid or taken to hospitals.

Tragically, several of the city's largest hospitals were among the most damaged buildings. At the Centro Medico y Mexico General Hospital, one of the largest medical complexes in Latin America, six buildings collapsed, killing approximately 1,200 people. At the nearby Juárez Hospital about 400 doctors, nurses, and patients were trapped when the floors beneath them collapsed into stacks of concrete.

Buildings damaged in the earthquake included apartment complexes, seven tourist hotels, 10 percent of the

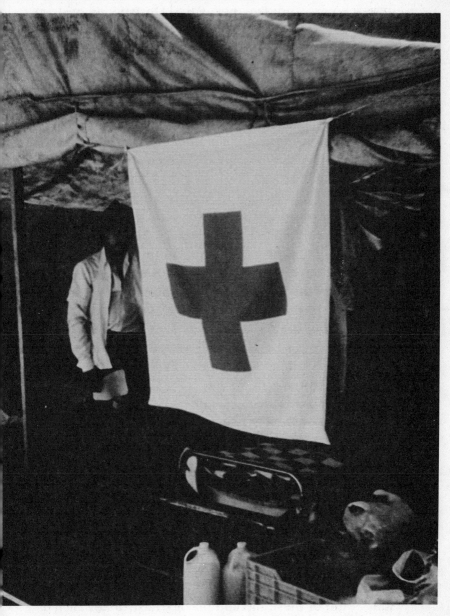

*The Red Cross set up temporary shelters to house some of the thousands of people made homeless by the 1985 Mexico City earthquake.*

city's schools, and five hospitals. Destruction was so widespread that it was difficult for officials to establish the total cost of the damage, although some estimates were as high as 5 billion dollars. International relief came from a variety of sources: the United Nations, individual governments, voluntary agencies, and the International Committee of the Red Cross. Gifts included cash and supplies such as food, clothing, vehicles and earth-moving equipment. Medical teams from the United States, Norway, France, and at least twenty-four other nations also arrived to join the relief effort. International contributions to Mexico City are estimated by the UN to have totalled more than 13 million dollars.

The first hours and days following a disaster—when people need food, temporary shelter, and urgent medical care—are the *emergency phase*. At this time a disaster is headline news. However, long after the disaster has faded from the public eye, its victims may still need assistance. This is called the *reconstruction period*, a time when disaster victims need help to rebuild, and return to a normal life.

Many different kinds of people help disaster victims. They include missionaries, social workers, psychologists, government and community groups, civilian volunteers, and professional disaster relief personnel. The following sections include information on relief organizations, whose programs help people who have suffered through natural disasters.

## The Red Cross

Each year the volunteers and workers of the Red Cross respond to an average of 40,000 disasters worldwide. Some of these include major catastrophes such as floods, hurricanes, tornadoes, volcanoes, chemical and nuclear accidents, as well as localized events like fires and transportation accidents. The Red Cross has the highest public profile of all disaster relief organizations; its flag, a red cross on a white background, is a familiar symbol of *nonpartisan* aid in time of crisis.

The Red Cross was founded in 1864 in Geneva, Switzerland, by Jean Henri Dunant, an influential Swiss philanthropist. Four years earlier, on a battlefield in Northern Italy, he had been shocked by the lack of care given to wounded soldiers. In Solferino, Italy, France and Italy were fighting the army of Austria. About 40,000 men lay dead or dying on the battlefield and thousands more lay wounded in the nearby town of Castiglione.

Soon after, he organized a civilian voluntary force to care for the wounded men. He commandeered travelers, priests, housewives, and anyone else who was willing to bind wounds and feed and comfort the injured. Not content with limiting his efforts to Italy alone, Dunant traveled all over Europe in an effort to enlist people in his campaign to assure better care for victims of war.

By October 1863, Dunant had helped set up an international conference with the aim of forming a volunteer, civilian organization to aid wounded soldiers. Thirty-six delegates from sixteen countries—including Switzerland, the United States, France, and England—attended this meeting. The group became known as the International Committee of the Red Cross (ICRC). Today, ICRC's main purpose is to treat people wounded by war and to protect prisoners of war and civilians in international and national conflicts. However, it is also involved in natural disaster relief. Most disaster relief is provided by local Red Cross chapters organized within member countries.

Shortly after the ICRC was formed, governments

around the world were invited to form their own national Red Cross societies. Today there are more than 125 such groups. Most use the red cross as their symbol. The cross resembling the Swiss flag in reverse colors, represents the Christian ideals of the society and is also a tribute to the organization's Swiss founder. However, in many non-Christian countries a symbol other than a cross is used. For instance, Iran uses a lion and rising sun; Israel incorporates the Star of David; and Moslem countries such as Saudi Arabia employ a crescent.

The Red Cross society in the United States is known as the American Red Cross (ARC) and has its headquarters in Washington, D.C. It was founded in 1881 by Clara Barton. Today, it is one of the world's largest societies with a staff of 17,000, 60 divisions, and more than 3,000 local chapters.

It is national Red Cross societies like the ARC that are mainly responsible for disaster relief, and public health and welfare. Each society conducts a variety of programs that best fit the needs and resources of its own country. Many societies train nurses aides, visiting housekeepers, and mothers' assistants. Others, such as the Iranian Red Lion and Sun and the Guatemalan Red Cross, maintain children's clinics. Some, such as the Indian Red Cross, train midwives. In many Latin American countries, the Red Cross operates hospitals, pharmacies, and mobile clinics. A federation called the League of Red Cross Societies, formed in 1919 and headquartered in Geneva, coordinates policies and activities of the national societies.

Through local chapters, the American Red Cross trains people in emergency care so that they can be called upon when a disaster occurs. Emergency assistance may include providing shelter, first aid, food,

clothing, financial assistance with rent, essential household goods, minimum home repairs, health needs, and
replacement of work supplies and equipment. The
American Red Cross has its own short-wave emergency
radio frequency to use when normal communication
lines are disrupted. The ARC also works with government and private organizations to put disaster victims in
touch with such groups when appropriate. When the
American Red Cross gives aid to people outside the
United States, it does so in conjunction with local Red
Cross groups. All aid provided by the American Red
Cross is free.

Although the American Red Cross receives its author-
ity from a charter granted from the United States Congress, it receives no direct funds from the federal government. Funding comes from direct donations; the
United Way, an organization that provides financial aid
to a number of health, welfare, and recreational agencies
through a single annual fund drive; foundation grants;
government grants and contracts for specific projects;
special events; and cost recovery fees. For large-scale
disasters, the Red Cross conducts special disaster fund
campaigns. In addition to paid staff members, the American Red Cross depends on 1.4 million volunteers to
perform a wide variety of jobs. These include collecting
and distributing blood, driving Red Cross vehicles, and
working in disaster situations.

In many countries the national Red Cross society
forms the keystone of a national disaster relief plan. The
Red Cross movement's independence from political ma-
nipulation, its national identity through local chapters,
and its training and support services that emphasize self-
help and voluntary help, make it one of the most effective sources of disaster relief. By having local people

*The Red Cross set up temporary shelters to house some of the thousands of people made homeless by the 1985 Mexico City earthquake.*

trained, a government can better manage its own relief operation when a disaster strikes.

*United Nations' Organizations*

Due to a series of devastating natural disasters that occurred in the late 1960s and early 1970s, the United Nations General Assembly created the Office of United Nations Disaster Relief (UNDRO) in December 1971. Although the international community had always responded with large amounts of relief aid, many efforts failed primarily due to supplies arriving late, unavailable specific information on what was needed, and problems with distribution of funds and provisions.

UNDRO functions in three ways: *Relief coordination,* which mobilizes and coordinates emergency action to provide services that are both timely and specific to the type of disaster and the country in which it occurs; *disaster preparation,* which implements programs to raise the level of disaster planning and preparatory measures, including assessment and relief management capability in developing nations that are disaster-prone; and *disaster prevention,* which promotes the study, prediction, and alleviation of natural disasters by collecting and distributing information on developments in technology and science. For instance, in 1987, UNDRO workers were involved in a number of relief efforts, including a project in El Salvador to rebuild a home for orphans and destitute women that had been destroyed by the 1986 earthquake. Long-term disaster relief projects in 1987 included a cooperative venture with the government of the Netherlands to prepare a manual on disaster prevention to be used by planners and builders in developing countries. Recently, UNDRO workers also presented papers at scientific meetings on the use of space technology for disaster warning and determining the effects of natural disasters.

In some cases UNDRO staff is sent directly to the countries struck by disasters. There, they are largely involved in assisting the government in assessment of damage and needs, as well as coordinating relief efforts by other UN agencies to avoid overlapping services.

As of 1985, UNDRO was allocated an operating budget of approximately 5.2 million dollars by the United Nations. However, the organization also depends upon donations by governments, private charitable groups, and individuals. The UNDRO Coordinator, who holds the rank of Under-Secretary General of the United Nations, has the power to allocate the UN budget as well as any voluntary contributions. Grants given to countries in distress are normally limited to $50,000, although emergency relief funds have been extended that are as high as $600,000 per year for a single nation in extreme need. Funds are used to provide food and technical assistance as well as for rebuilding homes, hospitals, and businesses.

UNDRO can only become involved in the coordination of disaster relief at the request of the government of the stricken country. Even then, actually getting relief supplies where they are most needed is difficult. *When Disaster Strikes*, an UNDRO publication, identifies some of the most disturbing obstacles to disaster relief, such as the bureaucratic, legal, and commercial procedures employed by governments. These may include delays in obtaining landing clearances for aircraft bearing supplies, entry visas for relief workers, or desirable exchange rates for relief units. Ultimately, the task of UNDRO's fifty member staff is to coordinate the activities of UN agencies with government, intergovernment, and volunteer agencies, to enable the most effective relief effort possible to take place.

Within the United Nations there are several agencies that provide important services in disaster situations even though their primary function is not disaster relief. The United Nations International Children's Emergency Fund (UNICEF) has continuing programs in many developing and underdeveloped nations. Therefore, when disaster strikes, they have the advantage of being able to provide immediate aid.

UNICEF concentrates on the special needs of children and young mothers. It provides health care, education, nutrition, clean water and sanitation equipment, family planning, children's mental health services, and improvement in the lives of women and girls. UNICEF plans, purchases, ships, and distributes a wide range of supplies to disaster areas. UNICEF relies on voluntary contributions from governments, private organizations, and individuals to fund its programs. In a recent appeal it solicited 13.7 million dollars for its emergency programs. Some of this money will help provide food, fuel, seeds, blankets, and clean water to starving families in Mozambique where drought has created severe food shortages. UNICEF has its main offices in New York, plus several regional centers and fifty field offices in other parts of the world.

Other UN agencies frequently involved with disaster relief are the Food and Agricultural Organization (FAO) and the World Food Program (WFP). The FAO gives advice on emergency preparation pertaining to food and nutrition. It also gives technical advice on rebuilding farms and food production facilities. Through its Global Information and Early Warning System, the FAO monitors the global food supply so that it can provide information to governments; oversees food supplies at the national level and tries to identify countries that face potential food shortages; and assists developing nations by helping them make decisions that will affect food supplies positively. The system is designed to help countries predict food surpluses as well as food shortages. Ironically, surplus food may create problems by driving the price of farm crops down or by discouraging farmers from planting new crops that lead to future food shortages. FAO-sponsored early warning projects are in operation or under preparation in countries in Africa, Asia, and Latin America.

The WFP provides emergency food and sometimes helps local governments to distribute it. Recent emergency operations include supplying food for refugees in Kampuchea, Pakistan, Somalia, and Zimbabwe; for drought victims in Mozambique and Nepal; and for the victims of floods and caterpillar infestation in Guinea.

The World Health Organization (WHO), whose primary objective is the attainment of the highest possible level of health for all people, provides advice to local governments on public-health issues related to disasters. For instance, when an earthquake destroys clean water supplies or sanitation systems, WHO gives advice on preventing the spread of disease or epidemics. In some cases, WHO ships medical equipment and supplies to disaster areas. Other UN agencies such as the International Telecommunications Union (ITU), which conveys messages, and the World Meteorological Organization (WMO), through its Weather Watch program, can also become involved in disaster relief or disaster warning. The World Weather Watch program, which is based on a system of satellites, regional weather centers, and national weather services, provides its members with information that enables them to operate efficiently and make local and specialized forecasts.

## Government Agencies

When a disaster strikes a community, local, state, and federal government agencies are among the first to respond. Emergency teams of fire, police, and health-care personnel are trained to deal with crisis situations. In a major disaster, members of the armed forces or, as in the United States, the National Guard, may be called upon to keep order and give emergency aid.

Many countries have provisions in the national budget for disaster relief. In 1970, the U.S. Congress passed the Disaster Relief Act to provide government funds to victims of disasters in the United States. If a community is declared a national disaster area by the president, citizens may be eligible for financial aid and low-interest loans to help them during the reconstruction period to rebuild their homes and businesses. In 1973, the Flood Disaster Protection Act amended and enhanced the 1970 *Disaster Relief Act* by making more assistance available to victims of disasters such as floods and tornadoes.

When a disaster occurs in another country, particularly in a developing or underdeveloped nation that may not have the money or resources to deal with the emergency, the government may solicit help from other nations. For instance, when Mexico City was struck by its earthquake, the national government, already burdened by foreign debt and a depressed economy, did not have the resources to pay for the recovery. Even with help from other countries, the Mexican economy was severely set back by the earthquake, and today there are still portions of the city that have not been rebuilt.

The United States government, like the governments

of many other nations, has funds from which they can make direct contributions of money to aid disaster victims in other parts of the world. One of the primary agencies providing international disaster relief in the United States is the Agency for International Development (AID). AID was established in 1961 by President John F. Kennedy and is a unit of the U.S. Department of State. It operates chiefly through loans and grants to less developed countries and its purpose is to promote social and economic development. Countries that receive aid must do long-range planning, establish self-help programs, and try to work toward self-support. AID's office of Foreign Disaster Assistance provides international disaster relief. Other countries with similar governmental offices designed to deal with foreign disaster aid are Great Britain, France, Sweden, Australia, New Zealand, and Canada.

## Private Organizations and Voluntary Agencies

Although the majority of the money that goes to disaster relief in the United States and elsewhere is provided by direct government contributions, the private sector and volunteer groups play an important role as well. Because they are smaller and less bureaucratic than governments, they are often able to get into action more quickly. If they are already on the spot, as many church groups are, they can begin work immediately.

Church groups are traditional providers of charity to the poor and the needy. Because it is part of Christian doctrine to care for others in distress, church workers and missionaries are among the oldest organized relief groups. Although indoctrination with Christian beliefs is usually the ultimate goal of mission workers, the provision of food and health care is often the primary service

*Farmers in Brazil await rescue during disastrous floods in 1979. AID and the American Red Cross rushed in relief supplies that were transported by the US Air Force and the Brazilian Air Force and Navy.*

performed. Thus, in developed and developing countries, where many churches have missions, these groups are frequently the best prepared to offer help when a disaster strikes.

Private groups may be able to provide assistance in places and at times when government organizations cannot do so for political reasons. For instance, in Biafra in 1969 and 1970, it was not possible for outside government agencies—which needed to operate through official channels—to provide aid to starving children because of the war, whereas private groups did not need official approval. Private groups also have the advantage of being more flexible than the larger relief organizations and can bypass bureaucratic "red tape."

One of the biggest problems with disaster relief efforts is coordinating the various groups. In 1972, five of the major agencies met in Geneva and decided to form a central coordinating body called the Steering Committee. The Steering Committee consults regularly on the current relief operations of its members. It also has collated and summarized all existing national disaster plans, drawn up country profiles of disaster-related information on developing nations, and completed an inventory of world-wide university faculties doing disaster-related research and teaching. During a relief operation, members of the Steering Committee keep in touch with UNDRO, and UNDRO cables situation reports to them. Members of the Steering Committee are the Oxford Committee for Famine Relief (OXFAM), Catholic Relief Services (CRS), the World Council of Churches (WCC), the Lutheran World Federation (LWF), and the League of Red Cross Societies.

OXFAM began in England in 1943 and provides disaster assistance world-wide. United States' offices are in

Boston. It supports programs that study the underlying causes of disaster and provides money for self-help projects in underdeveloped countries in Asia, Africa, and Latin America. It also responds to emergency needs after a disaster, with food, water, and medical care. OXFAM funds come from thousands of individual donors and from a network of secondhand shops staffed by 15,000 unpaid volunteers.

The WCC is an ecumenical fellowship of 301 Protestant, Anglican, Old Catholic, and Orthodox churches in 100 countries and territories. It conducts a wide range of programs including refugee aid and disaster services. It was founded at an assembly of representatives in Amsterdam in 1948 and has offices today in New York and Geneva, Switzerland.

The CRS is a non-political, non-evangelical, official overseas relief and self-help development agency of the American Catholic community. Its programs include disaster aid, refugee relief, and rehabilitation. It distributes food, clothing, and medicines to the needy. Except for the Red Cross, the Catholic Relief Services is the world's largest private relief organization, with 200 staff members in the United States and 150 overseas. In addition, 725 people work in local groups abroad.

The LWF and its subcommittee, Lutheran World Relief, serve the Lutheran churches of the United States in overseas programs of community development, social service, and material aid. Its programs extend to Asia, Africa, and Latin America; it also assists other relief agencies in case of a disaster.

The Steering Committee operates as an information exchange. The members consult with each other regularly and because each member is also the center of its own large relief network, the influence of the committee is wide. In a particular disaster, it allows members to compare information on the extent of damage, number of victims, what they need, the amount of relief provided, and transport problems.

In every country there are hundreds of private organizations that provide relief for disasters. Some, such as CARE and Save the Children, operate independently, whereas others, such as Church World Service and Caritas Internationalis, are linked to members of the Steering Committee.

CARE, which stands for the Cooperative for American Relief to Everywhere, Inc, was founded in 1945 by a group of twenty-five smaller relief agencies for the purpose of sending food and clothing to needy people in Europe after World War II. Today it is an international public service and development organization providing food, self-help development, disaster aid, and health-care training in thirty-seven developing countries in Asia, Africa, the Middle East, and Latin America. It has a staff of 436 and maintains committees of volunteers in many U.S. cities. CARE is supported by contributions from American, Canadian, and European individuals, and from governments and private organizations.

The U.S. government provides Food-for-Peace agricultural products and financial grants for emergency relief and development programs. Host governments share in operating costs and often supply local staff members. CARE focuses on nutrition and nutrition education. In 1962, Medical International Cooperation Organization (MEDICO) became a service of CARE. It supplies teams of physicians, nurses, and medical technicians to hospitals and clinics in developing countries and trains native health care workers.

Church World Service is part of the Division of Overseas Ministries of the National Council of Churches of Christ in the United States and provides world-wide aid to the needy. It extends relief, supplies, technical assistance, reconstruction and inter-church aid, and ministers to the victims of war and other emergencies such as famines and floods. It sends food, clothing, medicines, hospital supplies, blankets, and self-help equipment overseas to over seventy countries.

Save the Children helps needy children by improving the communities in which they live. It sponsors programs in the United States and seventeen other countries. Save the Children projects include nutrition and health programs, and the building of homes, roads, schools, and water systems. The organization was founded in 1932 and is headquartered in Westport, Connecticut.

Caritas Internationalis (International Confederation of Catholic Organizations for Charitable and Social Action) operates both nationally and internationally in the fields of education, social welfare, medicine, international relations and aid to less-developed countries. It was founded in 1950 with headquarters in Rome and today has member organizations in 113 countries. Permanent delegations in New York, Geneva, Paris, Rome, Strasbourg, and Vienna cooperate with the United Nations and its specialized agencies. In cases of disasters in member countries, its role is to stimulate and coordinate relief efforts. Its budget for development, social welfare, and emergency aid in 1980 was 120 million dollars.

## The Media

Daily newspaper headlines and prominent news stories on television and radio frequently feature reports on major disasters. There is an old saying that bad news travels fast, and people always seem to be fascinated by scenes of death and destruction. While these news reports are horrifying, they serve a greater purpose of informing the public and motivating sympathy for the disaster victims. Sometimes there are cases where zealous news reporters have kept disasters in the public eye, and consequently, relief programs were mobilized. For instance, a recent year-long series of reports on the Ethiopian famine by the magazine *Stern* was instrumental in influencing the West German government's contribution of more than 10 million dollars to the relief effort. On the other hand, the sheer number of disaster reports can numb the public consciousness, so that, unfortuantely, only disasters of gigantic proportion have an impact.

The media also plays an important role in evaluating relief efforts and focusing information; in some cases, they have even mounted their own relief efforts. After the 1985 Mexico City earthquake, a Spanish language television station in Los Angeles, KMEX, organized a telethon that raised more than 5 million dollars. In 1972, after Hurricane Agnes devastated much of the eastern United States, twenty television stations donated air time for the Bob Hope American Red Cross Celebrity Flood Relief television special to raise money for the victims.

Each type of natural disaster has its own special causes and results. In each of the following chapters, there is one example of a particular type of natural disaster that includes some of the ways in which organizations and individuals responded and descriptions of circumstances that befell the victims.

# CHAPTER TWO

# Hurricanes and Floods

For ten, terrible days in June 1972, Hurricane Agnes churned across the eastern United States, dumping billions of gallons of rain water into already overflowing rivers and creeks. By the time the rains stopped, the hurricane had flooded 4,500 miles of rivers and 9,000 miles of streams, causing water damage in 25 cities and 142 counties in 5 states. More than 5,000 square miles of land were covered with water, and over 330,000 people were homeless. According to the National Weather Service, they were the worst floods in U.S. history.

Hurricane Agnes began as a storm near Cozumel Island off the Yucatan Peninsula of Mexico, then moved northward across the Gulf of Mexico toward Florida. In the Florida Keys, the hurricane produced tornadoes. Like most hurricanes, Agnes grew weaker as she moved over land, and as she churned across Georgia and the Carolinas she dropped huge amounts of rain. Agnes brought severe flooding to the area around Asheville, North Carolina, before moving on to Virginia, West Virginia, Maryland, the District of Columbia, New Jer-

*Next pages: Hurricane storm surge. Heavy waves generated by hurricanes can cause major damage to coastal communities.*

N.O.A.A.

sey, and, finally, into New York and Pennsylvania, where she caused record-breaking floods.

Agnes brought disaster to more than half a million Americans in the metropolitan areas of Richmond, Washington, D.C., Baltimore, Philadelphia, New York, Pittsburgh, and Rochester. She brought frightful devastation to the city of Wilkes-Barre and the Elmira-Corning areas and to more than 500 small communities from the Florida Keys to the south, Ohio to the west, and New York state to the north. In Wilkes-Barre, the Susquehanna River crested at 40 feet and washed over flood-control dikes, forcing over 100,000 people to flee their homes.

The American Red Cross reported that as a result of the storm, 117 people died and more than 15,000 were injured. Deaths were caused when people became trapped in raging flood waters and drowned, or when high winds toppled trees or buildings on top of them. Some people were killed when struck by pieces of lumber, panes of glass, roof shingles, or other wrecked objects swirling about in the flood. Other flood-related deaths included those caused by starvation, and disease caused by drinking or eating contaminated supplies of food and water.

Because of their size and duration, hurricanes and the accompanying floods can be the most destructive of all natural disasters. At its peak, a hurricane produces approximately 16 trillion kilowatt hours of energy per day, or the equivalent of a half million atomic bombs. This energy is released in heavy rainstorms and in the production of powerful sea waves. Hurricane waves can erode 30 to 50 feet of beach within an hour. Half a day of battering by hurricane waves is equal to a century's normal wave action. By the time most hurricanes reach inland areas, the wind has subsided, but the torrents of rain which the storm still carries often cause disastrous flooding, as in the case of Hurricane Agnes.

The general name for a hurricane, as it is called in the Atlantic, or a typhoon, as it is called in the Pacific, is a cyclone. Cyclones are large circular storms that originate over warm tropical waters. The diameter of the storm can vary between 50 and 1,000 miles, although usually it's range is 100 to 200 miles wide. A cyclone's center, or "eye," is like the hub of a giant wheel with strong winds swirling around it. As these winds reach 74 or more miles per hour, the storm is classified as a hurricane. Hurricane winds have been measured at up to 175 miles per hour, and some may be even stronger.

In coastal areas, damage from hurricanes comes from high winds, driving rains, and powerful sea waves that surge onto the shore. In a disastrous hurricane in September 1900, pounding waves literally swept away the coastal city of Galveston, Texas, killing 6,000 people.

Although the people in Galveston had been warned of the approaching storm and told to evacuate, many remained behind. As the winds rose to hurricane velocity, the only bridge connecting Galveston to the mainland collapsed. As the rain poured down, the high winds blew about shingles and loose timbers. Most people gathered in the center of town and took refuge in the highest-story hotel. By then the water in the streets was four feet deep and rising fast. As the water rose, the tide—more than 20 feet above normal—swept into the city. Houses were torn from their foundations and pushed by the surging water against other buildings, knocking them down. Thousands of people were killed by drowning or by being struck by flying objects. Most of those who survived did so by clinging onto floating

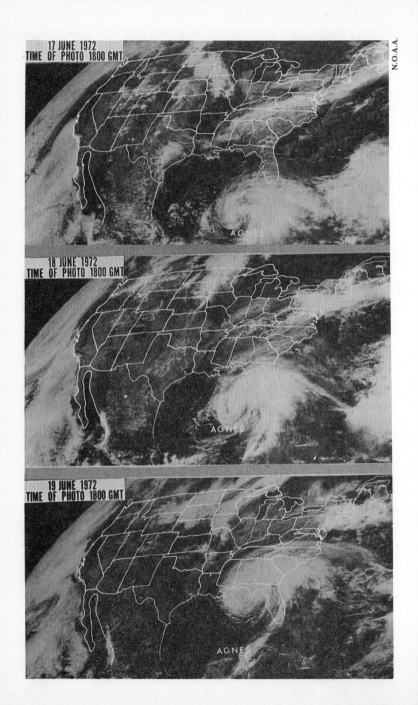

debris until the storm subsided. All that could be seen above the surface of the water were the tops of a few of the strongest and tallest buildings. As I. M. Cline, the director of the weather bureau and a survivor of the storm wrote later, "Where 20,000 people lived on the 8th, not a house remained on the 9th." The city had been completely destroyed.

A hurricane storm system starts in the tropics and moves northward about 200 miles per day, sometimes traveling 1,500 to 2,000 miles before subsiding. Each year there are about eight to ten tropical storms big enough to be called hurricanes by the U.S. Weather Bureau. The storms are identified by names that have been selected ahead of time and are assigned alphabetically. Until the late 1970s, all hurricanes had female names, but today male and female names alternate.

Satellite photographs of storm clouds depict hurricanes as giant pinwheels hanging above the earth. Unlike most other natural disasters, hurricanes can be identified as they are forming, with probable paths predicted. This allows people time to prepare for the storm and evacuate if necessary.

When Agnes' fury struck, the American Red Cross was standing by ready to help the hurricane's victims. As the storm moved northward, 122 chapters went into action. Local Red Cross volunteers worked with police, civil defense groups, fire departments, the National Guard, and many community groups to provide emergency aid. As the storm spread, 668 Red Cross shelters were opened—housing 178,000 people, feeding more than 500,000, and providing first aid or other forms of

*Opposite: Satellite photos show the path of Hurricane Agnes as it moved northward toward the Florida coast.*

care. In Wilkes-Barre, Pennsylvania and the Elmira-Corning area of New York State, so many people had lost their homes that some Red Cross shelters stayed open for two months.

Over 63,000 families received some kind of help from the Red Cross. A typical case was that of Gregg and Lisa Campbell (not their real names) and their three children, Jennifer, age seven, Christopher, age four, and Andrew age seven months. As the heavy rain pounded on the roof of their northern Pennsylvania home, they could see the water in the creek bordering the rear end of their property surging over the bank. As the water spread rapidly across their yard toward their house, Gregg began to place what furniture he could on top of tables and counters. Lisa helped the children put on their coats and boots and hurried them out to the car. In a few minutes they all left to go to a nearby school that had been converted into a temporary shelter.

The Campbells were forced to leave almost everything they owned behind—furnishings, clothes, and personal mementos. At the shelter the Red Cross provided them with cots and blankets, a change of clothing (theirs had gotten wet on the way to the shelter), diapers for the baby, and food. A nurse treated a small cut on Christopher's knee, but otherwise they were physically unharmed. A Red Cross volunteer registered the Campbells so their whereabouts would be known if anxious relatives inquired about their safety. An extemely distressing situation for relatives of disaster victims is not knowing whether their relatives are safe or alive.

Many other families had also sought shelter at the community center that night. For the children, the experience seemed rather like an adventure, but for the adults there was great concern as to how they would be able to recover or replace their belongings once the storm was over.

Two days later, the Campbells returned to inspect their home and found everything covered with mud. Although it looked as if the house could be cleaned up and made livable again, all their clothing and household furnishings were ruined.

At the local Red Cross Service Center, the Campbells met with a case worker to find out what kind of assistance could be provided. Because it would take at least several weeks to get their house in working order, the case worker helped the Campbell family obtain funds for one month's rent in a nearby apartment, new clothing, and a supply of food. She also urged the family to contact the federal government regarding their qualifying for a low-interest loan to repair or rebuild their home.

As the Campbell family left the interview they were given a cleaning kit containing disinfectant, a broom, bucket, shovel, soaps, and other items. They brought the items home, and began cleaning and getting their lives back to normal. Later, when the family was able to move back home, the Red Cross supplied basic goods such as beds, bedding, towels, and cooking and eating utensils. They also helped them with the down payments on basic appliances including a stove, refrigerator, and washing machine.

The Campbells had been able to salvage some of their clothes and furniture, but many of their belongings had to be thrown away. New appliances had been delivered and the food replaced in the kitchen cupboards. A loan from the government would help them pay the unexpected expenses.

The response to Hurricane Agnes was one of the largest relief efforts ever mounted by the American Red

*Heavy rainstorms can trigger mudslides such as this one which buried a house and a car in Southern California in 1978.*

Cross. Most of the 20,000 workers were volunteers, including 3,000 nurses and other health-care personnel. They were supported by 1,300 professional Red Cross staff members. All worked tirelessly. Many other groups also gave assistance to flood victims. These included federal, state, and local governments; organized labor; community groups; and many churches.

In Wilkes-Barre, a group of volunteers from the Mennonite church devoted their Fourth of July holiday to helping flood victims. Armed with shovels, brooms, and buckets, they worked at removing the incredible mountains of debris left by the flood. Literally tons of waterlogged furnishings were hauled from houses. People swept, shoveled, and scrubbed away mud that caked the walls of the first and second floors of many homes. Like other volunteers in the gigantic relief effort, the Mennonites gave generously to those in need.

The total effect of disastrous floods such as those resulting from Hurricane Agnes is difficult to determine exactly. It is estimated that the storm caused over 3 billion dollars in property damage. The American Red Cross reported that it spent 23 million dollars on the relief effort. For everyone affected it was a major disruption of normal life, and for some it left scars lasting long after the visible mess was cleaned up. Tragically, some victims lost friends and relatives. For many people it also meant losing homes and other property as well as jobs. Factories and other businesses were forced to shut down for repairs or for good.

Hurricanes are a perpetual threat to people living in coastal areas. Although many hurricanes have wreaked havoc in the Atlantic region, the worst hurricanes in the world have been in the Pacific. More hurricanes form each year in the southeastern portion of the North Pacific than anywhere else in the world, with the most destructive storms in the Bay of Bengal. Because of the funnellike shape of the bay, the force of a storm is concentrated as it moves north along the coast of India toward Bangladesh. Some of the worst hurricanes in history have occurred in this area, including the cyclone of 1970 that devastated the low coastal plains of Bangladesh, killing more than a quarter of a million people.

Although scientists are studying hurricanes and learning more about how they work, there is still no way to prevent them. However, loss of life and some types of property damage caused by hurricanes can be prevented. In Bangladesh for instance, plans have been made to provide a better early warning system and to create large earthen hills as refuges in time of flooding. In other cases, as in Galveston, Texas, sea walls were built to provide a barrier against the waves.

For inland areas, flood control programs, strict building codes for low-lying areas, and adequate warning systems can help minimize the effects of floods. The United States has a national program of flood protection that includes the construction of *levees* and *flood walls*, the widening and deepening of river channels, and the creation of *floodways* to bypass farmlands and cities. In large river valleys engineers have built dams and reservoirs to help control flooding. But when weather patterns contrive to pour more water into the system than the flood controls can handle, disaster strikes.

CHAPTER THREE

# Earthquakes

At 3:02 A.M., February 4, 1976, for 39 awful seconds, a violent earthquake struck the heavily populated Guatemala highlands, killing and injuring thousands of people as they were crushed by falling masonry. All major services were disrupted. Telephone and electrical lines broke down, sewage and water pipes cracked, bridges collapsed, and landslides blocked major highways.

People rocked in their beds. Those who tried to get out were thrown to the floor. When the shaking stopped, survivors stumbled out onto the streets to see what had happened. People like the Salazar family were lucky. Even though their house had collapsed and most of their possessions were destroyed, they were still alive and unhurt. Toppled structures and piles of debris were everywhere, but because it was still dark and all communication lines were down, it was hard to know how many people were affected.

As soon as the sun came up the next day members of a volunteer Guatemalan flying club took off to survey the countryside and assess the extent of the damage. When they returned their reports were grim. The earthquake damage covered an area of more than 3,500 square miles, with the worst damage concentrated in a triangular area bounded by Guatemala City, Tecpan, and Joyabaj. When a special mission of the Inter-American Development Bank, an international agency that finances development projects in Latin America, visited Guatemala a week later, it assessed the property damage at more than 650 million dollars.

Earthquakes like the one in Guatemala are a natural result of the movement of the earth's crust. Although we do not usually notice it, the earth's surface is constantly changing. *Seismologist* Paul Davis from the University of California, Los Angeles, describes the earth as a giant ball of melted rock with large pieces of solid rock floating over the top. It may also be thought of as a spherical jigsaw puzzle with moving pieces called continental *plates*. The study of how the plates move and connect is called *plate techtonics*.

Sometimes two of the earth's plates crash into each other and push up huge mountains. This is how the Himalaya mountain range in Asia was formed. Sometimes a plate will break apart forming a gap called a *rift*, such as the huge Rift Valley in East Africa. In other cases, when two plates meet, they just slide by each other like two giant ships at sea. In California, the Pacific plate is moving northward past the North American plate at about two or three inches a year. Sometimes, instead of slipping past each other, two meeting plates get stuck. Then pressure builds up as the forces try to push the plates past each other. When the pressure is great enough, they slip apart suddenly and create an earthquake.

Each year there are thousands of earthquakes. Most are so small that they cannot be felt. Only when an earthquake measures a magnitude of 2 on the Richter scale is it strong enough to be felt without special

*Little was left standing after the Guatemala earthquake of February 1976.*

instruments. The Richter scale, originally developed by American scientist Charles Richter in 1935, measures the amount of energy generated by an earthquake. Each unit on the scale is about sixty times greater than the previous one. An earthquake with a Richter rating of 7 is about 200,000 times as powerful as an earthquake with a Richter rating of 4. Usually it takes an earthquake of 6.5 or larger to cause major injuries to people and damage to property.

*Guatemala earthquake, 1976. Rescue workers search for victims trapped in the rubble.*

The Guatemalan earthquake of 1976 measured 7.5 on the Richter scale. It was so strong that trees were split in half and railroad tracks bent like hairpins, yet it lasted less than one minute. In the capital, Guatemala City, 58,000 houses were destroyed. Many of the victims were killed in their beds or injured as walls of their homes collapsed and heavy tile roofs fell on top of them. The widespread use of adobe as a building material in rural areas and in poor sections of the cities was largely responsible for these injuries and deaths. Although this brick-like substance appears to be sturdy, it crumbles easily when it is stressed.

In Guatemala City only two of its seven hospitals were able to operate fully after the disaster. Patients had to

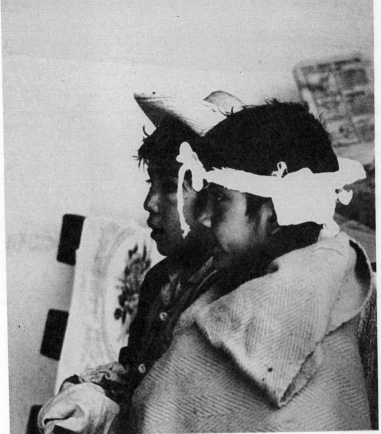

*Guatemala earthquake, 1976. Two young victims await medical care.*

be treated quickly and discharged to make way for new victims. Most hospitals were forced to move patients outside, as weakened structures crumbled further from aftershocks, the smaller earth tremors that frequently follow a large earthquake. A second, smaller earthquake occurred two days later on February 6, causing further damage with more than 1,500 additional after shocks

*Guatemala earthquake, 1976. Adobe bricks, a common construction material, became lethal weapons as walls tumbled down during the earthquake.*

occurring during the next six weeks. When authorities assessed the damage from the earthquakes they found that nearly 25,000 persons were killed, over 77,000 injured, and more than a million had lost their homes.

Within hours after the first tremor, the Guatemalan government and its citizens were mobilizing emergency care. This was done primarily through the National Emergency Committee (NEC), an office established in 1969 to coordinate disaster relief. At first the NEC set up four warehouses at the airport to store donations of food, clothing, medicines, and building material. Fortunately, despite some damage by the earthquake, the airport was still able to receive supplies. Then, in conjunction with U.S. personnel and members of the Venezuelan Civil Defense Group, who had arrived to assist the relief operation, the NEC set up a flight coordination center at the airport to send relief supplies via helicopter to areas that were otherwise inaccessible.

Another major relief effort was undertaken by the U.S. Agency for International Development (AID). It had a stockpile of relief supplies including food, tents, and medical supplies stored nearby in the Panama Canal Zone. These were rushed to the scene of the worst damage.

Many other government agencies contributed to the Guatemalan relief effort. U.S. helicopters played an essential role in carrying supplies and moving people, since most roads were not usable. U.S. Army radios were an important part of the emergency communication network, and often were the only way for remote areas to get news from the outside world.

On February 11, eight U.S. Special Forces contact teams were sent out to the most isolated villages. Each team included a medical corpsman, a radio operator, and a soldier from the Guatemalan Army. In one week they were able to visit 140 villages, treating nearly 800 people and evacuating 25 who were seriously injured.

In the region of Chimaltenango, which was almost totally destroyed, the U.S. government set up a one hundred-bed field hospital. Medical services were provided by U.S. Army personnel and a Nicaraguan Army medical team.

One of the most urgent needs in the emergency phase of the Guatemalan disaster was for safe drinking water. The earthquake had ruptured water and sewage lines that lay side-by-side so that sewage was leaking into the water and contaminating it. To solve this problem, the Thirtieth Engineer Detachment of the U.S. Army brought in several large water purification devices called *erdalators*. Each erdalator could produce 6,000 gallons of clean water per hour. The water was then put into 400 gallon tanks and distributed by helicopter throughout the country.

The emergency phase of the earthquake lasted about two or three weeks. Later, relief efforts were aimed at rebuilding the country. Many groups, both governmental and private, helped at this stage. The total value of U.S. government assistance to Guatemala was over 42 million dollars with an equal amount coming from private U.S. disaster relief agencies. The international community donated over 72 million dollars in disaster aid.

On April 21, 1976 the U.S. Congress enacted the Guatemala Relief Rehabilitation Act to provide 25 million dollars for disaster aid. Much of the money was used to rebuild roads and to purchase building materials for new homes and schools. In cases where families had lost everything they owned, items such as tool kits, wheelbarrows, shovels, and picks were provided.

*Guatemala earthquake, 1976. Women in Guatemala City neighborhood of 5,000 inhabitants get water at one of two working faucets in the entire neighborhood.*

To avoid such terrible destruction in future earth-quakes, the people were encouraged to build their houses from earthquake-resistant materials, such as wood and corrugated metal, which bend but do not usually break when stressed. Through cooperative efforts between the Guatemalan government and the AID program, 650,000 sheets of corrugated metal roofing were made available in rural areas and sold at reduced prices.

Despite the fact that the roofing was inexpensive, about 25 percent of the Guatemalan people still could not afford to buy it. To solve this problem, a system was set up to reinvest the proceeds from the sheet metal sales in community work projects such as the building of schools and community centers. With money they earned from working on these projects, earthquake victims could afford to buy their own construction materials. These programs helped Guatemalan citizens rebuild their communities while enabling them to establish their independence.

Governments from all over the world and many private relief agencies donated time, money, and goods to the Guatemalan relief effort. In the United States, many of the donated supplies were channeled through New Orleans. Here, items were cataloged and sorted before being shipped. For three months, volunteers sorted an estimated ninety-seven million tons of clothing, canned goods, and medicines. Several steamship lines transported the supplies free.

One of the problems in mass outpourings of gifts in times of crisis is that people sometimes donate inappropriate or unusable items such as frozen TV dinners or outdated canned goods. Often the best contribution to disaster victims is cash. It can then be used to buy whatever is needed most, which could be food, hospital supplies, or earthmoving equipment. Another problem is making sure that donated items reach the intended recipients. Routing and transporting goods is one of the most valuable roles of some relief agencies.

Throughout the world thousands of earthquakes occur each year. Of these, about 6,000 are strong enough to be felt by people, and about 800 are strong enough to cause damage to buildings. At least twenty are big enough to destroy a major city. Fortunately, most large earthquakes occur in remote earth and sea locations far from where people live. However, those earthquakes that do strike inhabited areas cause terrible destruction, killing an average of 15,000 people each year.

Earthquakes are the most deadly of natural disasters and are responsible for almost 50 percent of twentieth-century calamities in which 10,000 or more people have died. Mexico City lost nearly 7,200 people in 1985. A year later, more than 400 lost their lives in the October 1986 earthquake in San Salvador. The most destructive earthquake in the United States was in San Francisco in 1906 where over 300 people were killed.

Although most earthquakes in the United States occur in Alaska and California, no state is immune to the threat of earthquakes. Since 1700, more than 1,000 earthquakes have been reported east of the Mississippi River, many of them in the northeast. Outside of California and Alaska, damaging earthquakes have occurred in Charleston, South Carolina (1886–87), New Madrid, Missouri (1811), and Hebgen Lake, Montana (1959).

Unlike floods or hurricanes, it is almost impossible to know exactly when an earthquake will strike, so it is difficult to warn people to go to a safe place ahead of time. Scientists all over the world are trying to learn

*Above: The March 1964 earthquake in Alaska shattered the earth and rocked houses off their foundations.*

*Opposite: Lopsided houses after the San Francisco earthquake of 1906.*

more about earthquakes. In the United States these include university researchers, workers for the U.S. Geological Survey, a government agency that makes studies of the land and its resources, and scientists working for private corporations. Using sophisticated equipment such as laser beams or other devices called *creepmeters* that can detect very small changes in the earth, the scientists can monitor movements along fault lines. Data collected along the San Andreas fault in California indicate that there is a 50 percent chance of a catastrophic earthquake somewhere in southern California in the next 30 years. However, the exact place and time is impossible to predict. Perhaps someday they will be able to predict when and where an earthquake will occur. In the meanwhile, strict building codes in earthquake-prone areas and a knowledge of emergency procedures in the event of a disaster are the best preparation for coping with the next earthquake.

# CHAPTER FOUR

# Tsunami

On the night of May 23, 1960, in the city of Hilo, Hawaii, a wail of sirens pierced the air, warning citizens to evacuate their homes and go to higher ground. Thousands of miles away an earthquake on the Chilean coast had triggered a huge ocean wave called a tsunami. With gathering speed the wave was racing across the Pacific, crashing into islands and coastlines along its way. Hilo had been devastated fourteen years earlier by a series of 50 foot tsunami waves, so its citizens were prepared for the worst.

When the first wave struck the harbor at 9:00 P.M., the water was only four feet above normal, and there was no danger. However, by the time the second tsunami arrived at 12:40 A.M., the water had risen to 9 feet above normal. Even so, there was no significant damage. Then, less than a half hour later, a vertical wall of water over 20 feet high came rushing forward at 440 miles per hour. It crashed through the sea wall and buffer zone in the harbor and roared into downtown Hilo. Within seconds, the power plant was destroyed, plunging the city into darkness, and the pounding waves quickly destroyed 230 buildings.

When the water receded, the city streets were strewn with tons of garbage, fish, mud, and the wreckage of

*Tsunami damage in Hilo, Hawaii, 1960.*

small boats. The force of the water had shattered buildings, wrapped cars around tree trunks, and flattened
parking meters. Sadly, sixty-one people died; despite
warnings many had remained, either due to disbelief or
in the hope of seeing some excitement.

Tsunami is a Japanese word that describes the extremely long and low ocean waves that are created by
earthquakes, landslides, volcanoes, and undersea explosions. Sometimes tsunami are incorrectly called tidal
waves. *Tidal waves* are large waves caused by the moon's
gravitational pull on the earth. As the earth spins on its
axis, the moon pulls at the sea, causing it to rise on the
side closest to the moon and to a lesser degree on the
opposite side of the earth. These waves are usually not
more than a few feet high unless there is a storm or an
unusual weather condition.

A tsunami is a single wave that may be 100 miles wide
from crest to crest and can travel great distances from its
source. A tsunami travels quickly, gaining speed in deep
water, sometimes going as fast as 650 miles per hour.
On the open sea, a tsunami is hardly noticeable. However, as it approaches shallow water it slows down,
building a wall of water at the front. When it crashes
against a distant shore its height may be between 50 and
100 feet.

A tsunami can travel great distances—up to 12,000
miles—without losing its force. In 1946 an earthquake
in Alaska created a tsunami that traveled southward, first
causing damage in Santa Cruz and Half Moon Bay in
California, and then, 5 hours later, in the Hawaiian
Islands.

*Next pages: Tsunami damage at Port Seward, Alaska, March 1964.*

*Tsunami warning sign on Hawaiian coast.*

The reason that tsunami cause so much damage is their tremendous force. A 30 foot tsunami exerts 49 tons of pressure per square yard. The greatest danger is along low sloping coast lines in curved bays or valley *fjords,* although any coast line less than 50 feet above sea level is vulnerable.

Usually a tsunami strikes in the form of a single large wave, although a series of waves is not uncommon. The wave travels outward from its source, in much the same way that the ripples spread when a pebble is dropped into a pond.

Tsunami are most common in the Pacific Ocean because of the regular undersea earthquake activity there. Since 1800 at least one tsunami a year had been recorded, although highly destructive waves only occur about once every ten years. In 1964, an earthquake in Alaska generated a tsunami that devastated the harbor at Port Seward, washing huge ships onto the mainland.

The highest tsunami ever recorded was a 210 foot wave that washed over the Kamchatka Peninsula on Russia's Pacific coast in 1737. However, the most deadly tsunami followed the gigantic volcanic eruption of the volcanoes on the island of Krakatoa in Indonesia on August 27, 1883, causing over 35,000 deaths in the South Pacific, wiping out much of the population of Java and Sumatra. As the giant wave rolled eastward, it went across the Indian Ocean, around the Cape of Good Hope and 4,700 miles into the Atlantic. Thirty-two hours later, a rise in the water level as far away as the English Channel was detected.

Tsunami waves cannot be prevented, but with proper community planning and an effective warning system, property damage and loss of life can be limited. For instance, today in Hawaii, building is severely restricted where tsunami are likely to strike. In Hilo, most of the low lying water front that was damaged so severely in 1946 and 1960 is now a park. Sensitive detection devices placed at strategic points in the ocean can provide early

*Liliakalani Park on Hilo Bay is now part of the buffer zone designed to protect the city from tsunami damage.*

warning of potentially dangerous waves. In the United States tsunami warnings are provided by the Seismic Sea Wave Warning System, a 24-hour early warning network for detecting earthquake activity around the Pacific Basin. It is part of a world-wide system called the International Tsunami Warning Center, which is part of UNESCO.

# CHAPTER FIVE

# Volcanoes

In central Colombia, high mountain ridges tower above fertile valleys below. Over the centuries the soil on the mountain slopes has become rich with volcanic ash and is ideal for growing coffee and rice. The people who live in the region are used to living in the shadow of disaster.

When Nevado del Ruiz, one of Colombia's two dozen active volcanoes, began ejecting large quantities of sulfuric gas in December 1984, it was the first sign of a possible eruption. In the following months a series of small earthquakes inside the mountain provided more evidence of volcanic activity and an explosion of steam and ash on September 11, 1985, indicated that pressure was building up. People had been living under this volcano for hundreds of years, but no one was prepared for the deadly consequences of the eruption of November 13, 1985.

On the afternoon of that day, about three o'clock, farmers working on the slopes of the mountain heard an explosion and saw a column of ash rise into the air. That evening the ash began falling on the streets of Armero, the largest town in the region. About an hour later a hard rain joined the falling ash and a strong smell of sulphur permeated the air. People wondered if they should evacuate their homes, but announcements over the radio and public address system assured them that

*Active volcanoes, like this one in Chile, are found throughout the Andes.*

there was no need to leave. Most people spent a quiet evening at home and went to bed early.

It was just after 10:00 P.M. that the mountain suddenly erupted again, sending a plume of fire and ash 25,000 feet into the air. As the ash rained down onto the town of Armero, citizens awoke and poured into the streets. What they didn't know was that the heat of the explosion had melted the ice cap that covered the 18,000 foot peak of the mountain, and a torrent of mud and water was rushing toward them.

On each side of the mountain the racing mud flows poured into river valleys and caused dams to break and rivers to flow over their banks. As the mud poured into the towns that bordered the rivers, it destroyed everything in its path, dragging with it people, cattle, tree stumps, giant rocks, and the remains of houses. Survivors said that the first wave was icy cold from the melted snow, but that the succeeding waves became warmer until they were burning hot. Unfortunately, most people became aware of the danger too late and were trapped in the gooey mud while trying to flee to higher ground.

The deluge buried almost all of the market town of Armero (population 25,000), and badly damaged several other smaller towns. Colombian authorities estimated that more than 25,000 people were killed, thousands injured, and up to 60,000 left homeless. It was one of the worst volcanic disasters in history.

As soon as the President of Colombia, Belisario Betancur, heard the news, he declared a state of emergency. Rescue crews from Colombia's Red Cross, the Civil Defense, the Armed Forces, and National Police were dispatched to help. One group of survivors was isolated on a small patch of land in the center of town that miraculously had been spared. Other survivors were

*Exhausted survivors of the November 1985 volcanic eruption in Colombia.*

stranded on roof tops, clutching tree branches, or half buried in mud.

In Armero, the mud spread over an area of 16 square miles. In some places it was 10 feet deep. Because the mud was so soft, the only way to reach most survivors was by helicopter or by building makeshift bridges over the mud. Helicopters hovered close to the surface, while rescuers lowered themselves with ropes and worked to free people. Because the suction power of the mud was so strong, rescuers had to be careful when extricating victims to avoid breaking their bones. One of the chief dangers for victims trapped in the mud was the loss of body heat that could lead to death from exposure. In one tragic case, a thirteen-year-old girl died from heart failure due to exposure, despite 60 hours of valiant efforts by rescue workers to free her.

When possible, the injured were transported to hospitals in nearby cities, but since most roads were blocked this had to be done by helicopters or airplanes. Instead, many people were treated in emergency hospital tents set up nearby. Because of the huge number of casualties, supplies ran low quickly and rescuers had to use whatever was available. Doctors worked around the clock, and in many cases had to use cardboard and masking tape to make temporary splints for broken bones. Hospital tents filled up so quickly that some patients had to be placed on stretchers on the ground. Many of the victims were unconscious; others had large, open wounds or exposed broken bones.

Among the first outsiders to respond to the disaster were the United Nations and the governments of the United States, France, Britain, Mexico, and six other nations. Within a day the United States was able to dispatch 12 helicopters, 500 family size tents, 4,500 blankets and other supplies that were stored in the Panama Canal Zone.

Most of the survivors were rescued during the first three days following the disaster. After medical care, the most urgent need for the victims was food and shelter. Refugee camps for survivors were set up in the nearby towns of Lerida and Guayabal. Almost everyone in Armero, and many in other towns had lost family members. Many children had suddenly become orphans.

Although some survivors were able to find homes with

*Colombia. Refugee camp for survivors of the volcanic eruption.*

*Opposite: Volcano, Colombia. Helicopters plucked survivors from the mud and carried them to dry ground.*

*Colombia. Red Cross food distribution at a refugee camp for survivors of the 1985 volcanic eruption.*

friends or relatives in other communities, and some were able to rebuild, nearly 4,000 were still living in refugee camps a year later. In a unique program operated by the American Red Cross, a group of young people from Los Angeles traveled to Colombia in August of 1985 to work with the Colombian Red Cross in the refugee camps. The volunteers helped distribute food, organized recreational activities for children, gave medical care, and taught courses in how to prepare for and respond to disaster. Normally Red Cross volunteers are recruited locally. This joint venture provided a rare opportunity for young people from the U.S. to interact with Red Cross volunteers in Colombia and share ideas and work together.

One question that was raised after the disaster of the Nevado del Ruiz eruption, was why people had not been warned to leave the area, particularly since the volcano had shown signs of imminent eruption for some time. Although the government had drawn up plans to prepare for disaster, they had never been put into effect. Armero's Civil Defense Committee had issued a warning to evacuate late on the night of the eruption, but most people ignored it. As one member stated later, "The people didn't leave. They were used to living with the problem and they didn't believe it." In any case, there was very little time, even for those who heeded the warning.

Following the disaster, geologists and volcano experts from all over the world came to study the volcano. Like earthquakes, volcanic eruptions are a natural consequence of changes within the earth. Deep inside the earth, under the hard outer crust, is molten rock. In some places, cracks or holes in the crust allow the hot rock, lava, gas or ashes to leak out. Sometimes lava leaks out relatively slowly as it does in the Hawaiian volcanoes. In other cases, it erupts with explosive force sending up showers of ash and molten rocks. The disaster in Colombia was actually a secondary result of such a violent eruption. The eruption itself was not deadly, but the accompanying landslide and heat that melted the snow was catastrophic. In other kinds of volcanic disasters people are killed by falling ash or from hot poisonous gases.

One of the most famous volcanic eruptions was at Mount Vesuvius in Italy in 79 A.D. For several days the mountain spewed forth lava and ash. The ancient Roman historian, Pliny the Younger, described the event in a letter. He wrote:

> A sudden and stupendous crash resounded, as if the whole mountain were caving in, first immense boulders flew up in the air as high as the crater edge, then came a huge fire and so much smoke that the whole sky went dark and the sun entirely disappeared as if in an eclipse.
> These events caused people to flee their houses for the streets and the streets for their houses; they fled the sea for land and the land for sea. In their terror they considered any place safer than where they happened to be.

When the eruption subsided, the ancient city of Pompeii was buried under 20 feet of ash; mud and lava had destroyed nearby Herculaneum, killing an estimated 20,000 people. Much of our knowledge of ancient Roman life comes from the archeological evidence buried at those two sites.

One of the biggest volcanic eruptions of all time occurred in 1815, when Mount Tambora in Indonesia threw so much ash into the air that it blocked out the sun for three days. In the following year the ash continued to cloud the atmosphere, contributing to the coldest year in modern history, sometimes known as the "year without a summer." That summer was so cold that it snowed in July. When nearby Krakatoa erupted in 1883, it exploded with a force of thirty hydrogen bombs. Its chief destructive force was in the giant tsunami it created.

At present there are about 500 to 600 active volcanoes world-wide. Most active volcanoes in the world are located on the edges of the Pacific Ocean in a circle known as the *Ring of Fire*. An active volcano is one that erupts on a regular or continual basis. Active volcanoes in the United States are in Hawaii, California (Mounts Shasta and Lassen), and Washington (Mounts Baker, St. Helens, and Rainier).

Many volcanoes go through long periods of dormancy between explosions, but when they do erupt, there is always the potential for great human disaster. Although it is unlikely that we will ever be able to prevent volcanic eruptions, the more scientists learn about volcanoes, the better they will be at developing advance warning systems.

# CHAPTER SIX

# Avalanches and Blizzards

Much of the world's population lives in areas where harsh winter weather is a fact of life. Most people cope with it by staying inside and dressing warmly when they go out. However, under extreme conditions, winter storms can develop into situations of potential disaster.

## Avalanches

Howling winds and driving snow had been pounding the high mountain ridges above the Alpine Meadows ski resort in the California Sierras for four days from March 26 to 29, 1982. Each day, 2 to 3 feet of new, wet snow was being piled onto the already heavy snow pack, steadily increasing the threat of a deadly avalanche. Although resort personnel were attempting to reduce the danger by setting explosives to trigger smaller, controlled avalanches, they could not keep up with the weather. By March 30, it was necessary to close the ski slopes to visitors, and by the next day all but a few of the staff were sent home. Those that remained included Anna Conrad, a ski lift operator, who had skied over to the resort with a friend from her house nearby, despite warnings from manager Bernie Kingery to stay away.

After being severely reprimanded by the manager for her recklessness, Anna went to look for her friend in the

*Alpine Meadows ski resort, March 1982, where an avalanche killed seven people.*

locker room of the ski hut. Suddenly, there was a huge roar as the building twisted and turned about her. Then, in the midst of a shrieking wind, the building exploded. Most of it was swept away in a giant racing wall of snow. The avalanche had struck, destroying nearly everything in its path, and Anna was trapped in a 2 foot high by 5 foot long cave formed by a bench and a toppled bank of lockers. There she remained for five days, until she was discovered by a heroic rescue team. Her experience is one of the most miraculous survival and rescue stories in avalanche history.

Strictly speaking, an avalanche can be the sudden slippage of a large amount of rock, earth, or snow. Nevertheless, most people think of avalanches only in terms of snow. Normally, new snow sticks to the snow beneath it. A snow avalanche begins when the snow mass on a mountain slope becomes overloaded with new snow, or when seeping rain or melted snow causes the bond with the slope beneath to loosen. Under such conditions the snow mass is extremely unstable and can become detached easily. An avalanche can be triggered by something as small as the weight of a single skier, the added weight of new snow, or perhaps a small earthquake.

An avalanche begins when a huge slab of snow cracks, breaks off, and starts to slide down the mountain. As it gains speed, it disintegrates into a river of flowing snow. Sliding on top of a thin ice layer underneath, the avalanche goes faster and faster, picking up more snow as it descends, sometimes reaching a total mass of a million tons. The roaring mass of snow may even become airborne. Without friction it can go even faster and may achieve a speed of up to 200 miles per hour. The force of some avalanches has been measured at 145 tons per square meter, forty-eight times the force needed to destroy a house. A descending avalanche also pushes forward a mighty air blast. Some avalanche experts believe that an air blast may have been the explosive force that caused the ski hut at Alpine Meadows to collapse.

When the avalanche struck at Alpine Meadows, eleven people were caught in its path. Seven of them died. The four who survived had all been inside the uppermost terminal building. Two of them were lucky to have been protected by the massive ski lift machinery, which shielded them from the onslaught of the snow. Randy Buck, a maintenance man, was able to dig himself out quickly and extricate Tad deFelice, who was also in the building, and Jeff Skover, who had been hurled out of the building and almost completely buried in the snow. Together the three men began to search for the others.

Within hours, news of the disaster spread and a search party that included 150 people and teams of specially trained search dogs was assembled. Both the danger of cold and suffocation made it crucial for the victims to be found quickly. If rescued within the first half-hour after being buried, a slide victim has a 50 percent chance of being found alive.

When Anna was struck by the lockers during the avalanche, she hit her head and fell unconscious. When she woke up several hours later, she was surrounded by darkness. For the next 24 hours she drifted in and out of consciousness.

Two days later Anna found some matches; she lit one and read the names on the lockers above her. At last she knew where she was and figured out what had happened. She realized her only chance for survival was to keep warm and to avoid becoming dehydrated by getting enough to drink. She pulled out all the clothes she could find from nearby lockers and put them on. Although there was no food, she found she could get water by eating snow. Then all she could do was wait and hope that someone would find her.

Above ground, the search party combed the area for any sign of the victims who they knew must still be buried in the snow. On Friday, April 2, a German shepherd dog named Bridget led the team to the site where Anna was hidden. Anna could hear them calling to her from above. Yet, despite her answering calls, they left. What Anna didn't know was that they could not hear her because the snowstorm had become much worse. The danger of more avalanches was considerable, and the search party was forced to leave. Two days later, however, the weather cleared and they returned.

Bridget again led the search team to the spot where Anna lay trapped below, and fifteen workers began to dig. Suddenly, Anna, whose strength was rapidly failing, saw a patch of light above her. Through the hole, snow began to drift in, and Anna grabbed at it thirstily. By then her own supply had run out, and she was beginning to become dehydrated. One of the workers saw her hand and shouted, "Anna is that you?" From deep in her hole, Anna shouted back joyfully. "I'm O.K. I'm alive."

The searchers could hardly believe their ears, to find Anna alive after so many days was almost a miracle. With great haste and enthusiasm, they dug away the remaining snow that covered the debris from the ski hut. Anna was given oxygen immediately. Finally, a wide enough entrance was made so she could be removed gently and lifted to a waiting helicopter that would fly her to a nearby hospital. As the helicopter rose the crowd cheered. Anna was lucky to have been found in time.

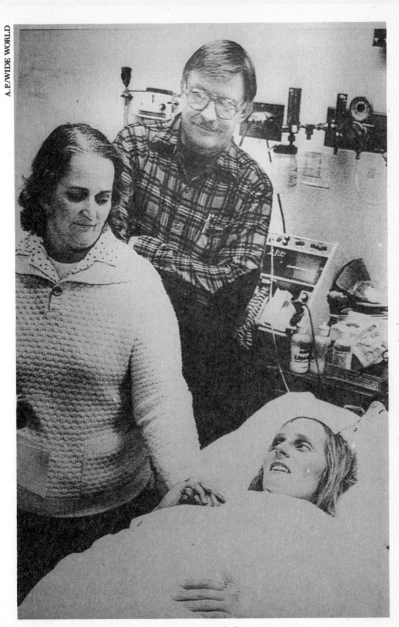

*Avalanche survivor Anna Conrad with her parents.*

Although there have been many terrible avalanches in history, relatively few people have died in them compared with the loss of life from other natural disasters. Most avalanches occur on high mountain slopes where few people live. The worst avalanche in recent times occurred in 1970 in Peru, when an earthquake triggered a massive snow and ice slide that obliterated the town of Yungay and killed its 18,000 citizens. During World War I, Italian and Austrian soldiers fighting in the Dolomite Mountains discovered that they could use gunfire to set off avalanches above enemy positions. An estimated 18,000 soldiers died in two days as victims of such avalanches.

Today gunfire and explosives are one technique of avalanche control. Setting off small avalanches can prevent a dangerous large one from building up. Another prevention technique is the building of large avalanche fences high on mountain slopes. This method has been used to protect some small mountain villages in Switzerland. Some buildings there are constructed with a large concrete wedge facing the mountain so that if an avalanche should come, the wedge will split it in two.

Despite preventative techniques, avalanches still occur. Rescuing avalanche victims has always been difficult. When an avalanche comes to an end, the snow packs itself into an ice-like density. For a victim trapped beneath such snow it may be difficult to breathe. Even when partially buried it is often impossible to get out of such snow alone.

Finding a buried avalanche victim is difficult, even with sophisticated scientific equipment. Until recently the best means of finding people buried in the snow has been with trained search dogs, such as the German shepherd that located Anna Conrad. A new method that helps protect people who go into avalanche-prone areas uses a small two-way radio called a transceiver. Each member of the group wears a transceiver and sets it on "transmit," which makes it emit a signal that can be heard by another transceiver set on "receiver." If one skier suddenly gets caught in an avalanche, the other members of the group quickly turn their transceivers onto "receive." By listening to the transmitted signal, which gets louder as they get closer to the source, they can quickly find their companion and dig him or her out of the snow.

## Blizzards

On the morning of March 12, 1888, residents of New York City opened up their newspapers and read the weather forecast, "Light snow, then clearing." It was one of the most erroneous weather predictions of the century. By the next morning, 24 inches of snow had fallen, and drifts 20 feet high blocked city streets, cutting off New York City and the surrounding suburbs from the outside world. Delivery wagons could not get through the streets and in many poorer sections of the city people went without food or coal to heat their homes. Four hundred people died from the extreme cold.

In February 1977, an unprecedented series of blizzards, combined with bitter cold temperatures, immobilized an estimated 75,000 citizens in western New York State. In Erie County, the Red Cross set up eighty-five shelter-feeding stations to service the storm-stricken community. The Red Cross provided shopping services for residents unable to leave their homes because of the snow, illness, or age, or due to the emergency travel ban that prohibited travel by all but emergency vehicles.

*Car buried by snowstorm, Adams, N.Y., 1977.*

Deliveries were made by volunteers in snowmobiles and four-wheel drive vehicles. U.S. servicemen from Fort Bragg were flown in to aid the National Guard with snow removal and other emergency services.

CHAPTER SEVEN

# Tornadoes

On the afternoon of April 3, 1974, the weather across the midwestern United States grew increasingly ominous. The humid air was oppressive, the wind was beginning to gust, and a menacing black cloud hung on the horizon. It was tornado weather. Within the next eight hours, a series of about 100 tornadoes, whirling funnels of violent wind, cut swathes across the land, destroying everything in their paths. When it was over, 400 million dollars worth of property was destroyed, and 350 lives were lost across a twelve-state-area. Red Cross statistics show that 95 shelters were opened in the 12 states suffering tornado damage, with 13,000 persons housed in shelters and over 250,000 fed. A total of 24,000 families suffered property losses.

One of the worst hit communities was Xenia, a town of 27,000 in southwestern Ohio. There, the ferocious winds ripped apart whole buildings and left them piled like matchsticks. Six of the town's twelve schools were destroyed or damaged, as were five of the seven supermarkets and hundreds of homes. According to news reports at least thirty died, more than 1,000 were injured, and half the city was leveled. Xenia's damage has been estimated at 100 million dollars.

Tornadoes are the most uniquely American weather disaster. Although tornadoes are occasionally reported in other continents, they occur by far the most frequently in the American Midwest, usually in an area called Tornado Alley. This region covers a broad area including Texas, Oklahoma, Kansas, Nebraska, and Arkansas, plus part of Louisiana, Missouri, Iowa, Colorado, Wyoming, and South Dakota. Other tornado pockets are in Georgia and Alabama, and in Illinois, Indiana, Michigan, and Ohio.

In the Midwest, tornadoes are formed when hot air from the Gulf of Mexico to the south meets cold air coming from the Rocky Mountains to the west. Normally, hot air rises and cools off, but when it becomes trapped under the layer of cold air, it cannot rise. If the hot air finds a "hole" in the blanket of cold air, it swirls upwards. As it rises, it cools, forming rain clouds. When these changes are rapid, a storm develops quickly, with dark skies, swirling rain and wind, hailstones, and thunder. At the center of the storm is the tornado, a funnel-shaped finger of swirling winds stretching from the high clouds to the ground.

The tip of a tornado can be as narrow as 3 yards or as wide as 2 miles, although most are about 250 yards in diameter. The tip of the tornado travels over the surface of the ground. It may go for a few feet or it may cut a path up to 50 miles long. The damage is caused by huge winds that swirl at up to 400 miles an hour around the core of the volcano. The tornado is like a giant vacuum cleaner that sucks up everything in its paths and then blasts it apart.

In Xenia, any property in the tornado's path was almost totally destroyed. Half the town was leveled when houses exploded. Those buildings that remained standing had all the windows blown out from the force of the wind. Metal signs were bent in half, trucks were blown into tree tops, and remnants of smashed buildings lay in rubble heaps on the ground. On top of the bowling alley roof sat a huge tractor trailer that had been lifted and dumped there by the wind. All over town gas, electricity, and telephone services were cut off, and dangerous live wires hung precariously from broken poles.

As soon as the storm subsided, the dazed survivors emerged to survey the wreckage. People who were injured were rushed to Miami Valley Hospital in nearby Dayton. President Richard M. Nixon declared Ohio and four other states national disaster areas. This meant that they would be eligible for federal money for immediate rescue and rehabilitation programs and for low-interest loans to help businesses reopen.

In Xenia, the Ohio National Guard came to the rescue with bulldozers, emergency rations, and medical supplies. Telephone and electrical workers rushed to restore services, and more than 800 Red Cross nurses and volunteers moved in to care for the injured and the homeless. Many people had lost everything they owned. One woman whose house was blown away described the remaining furniture as looking like a "pile of firewood."

One of the many groups to provide assistance to the tornado victims was the Salvation Army. In cooperation with the Federal Disaster Assistance Administration (FDAA), it provided food service at several evacuation centers and coordinated the distribution of food, blankets, and clothing.

For the first five days after the tornado hit Xenia, the Dayton Red Cross division headquarters remained open twenty-four hours daily to receive calls and to coordinate nursing activities around the town. Volunteer nurses were assigned to Red Cross shelters, where they administered medical aid. At one shelter, a pregnant mother

*Tornado damage in Xenia, Ohio, April 1974.*

had to be flown by helicopter to a hospital in Dayton to deliver her baby.

Many people in Xenia found it hard to grasp the scope of the destruction. One volunteer relief worker reported, "The devastation here is incredible. All that's left are concrete slabs and riddled shrubbery. What's left for the victim is a memory that won't erase easily."

In cooperation with the State Mental Health facilities the Red Cross provided "crisis prevention centers" and counseling services for people suffering from extreme emotional hardship. Red Cross social workers and psychologists also visited injured tornado victims in hospitals.

Throughout the Midwest other tornadoes had created scenes of havoc similar to that in Xenia. In Indiana, which also suffered an estimated 100 million dollars in property damage, the National Guard had to assign 1,000 men to the job of keeping sightseers out of the way. Every truck in the state that was still in working order was commandeered to help distribute needed supplies.

One of the worst things about tornadoes is their unpredictability, and when one does appear, there is little time to prepare. No one knows exactly where the tornado will touch down. It is almost impossible to protect a building that falls directly in the path of a tornado. When a tornado strikes, it may suddenly turn or go in circles, and its path varies in length from a few feet to many miles.

Tornadoes are also known for being strangely selective in their fury, destroying some objects while leaving others untouched. In one house in Xenia, one of the few objects left standing was the family's clothes dryer. Inside were broken dishes, tossed there by the wind, but on top of the machine sat a box of washing detergent exactly as it had been before the storm.

In the United States tornadoes kill about sixty-four people each year on an average. When an area is threatened by tornadoes, radio and television stations announce a tornado watch. Then, when a funnel is sighted, or when radar picks up an echo with the shape of a hook or a flying eagle, which are typical of a tornado-producing cloud, every means of communication is put into effect to warn people to take shelter immediately.

Since the mid 1960s the U.S. Weather Service has

kept a tornado watch over the midwestern United States, trying to predict the approach of tornadoes and to warn people who may be in their path. On days when weather conditions are favorable for tornadoes, the Weather Service alerts a volunteer network of ham radio operators know as the Radio Emergency Associated Citizen Team (REACT). These people take their equipment and move to spots with a good view of the surrounding area. If they spot a telltale funnel cloud, they alert local weather centers and civil defense and law enforcement authorities. Warnings are also broadcast to the public on radio and television and by alarm sirens.

Most tornadoes occur between the months of March and July, and usually strike between 4:00 and 6:00 P.M. The National Oceanic and Atmospheric Administration is working to provide a better early warning system for tornadoes so that people will have more time to find shelter. During tornado weather, it is important that emergency supplies are at hand. Listening to the radio is the best way to keep informed of any local changes in the weather.

CHAPTER EIGHT

# Forest Fires

On February 16, 1983, in a small town east of the Australian city of Melbourne, 120 children sat huddled under wet towels in their school's kindergarten room.

On the roof above them, their parents desperately sprayed water to prevent the school from catching fire. Around them blazed a terrible wildfire, one of the country's worst disasters. The blaze passed by them and the children and their parents were among the lucky ones to survive unharmed. Elswhere at least 71 people were killed and more than 1,000 injured. More than 3,000 square miles of valuable farm land was burned by the fire. Government officials estimated the damage to exceed 450 million dollars.

In Australia, where uncultivated land is called the bush, forest fires are referred to as bush fires. Bush fires have been a factor in Australian ecology for centuries, and many native plants, such as the huge eucalyptus trees which dominate the forests, are adapted to fire. They do not burn easily, and even when seriously scorched, they often revive. Although lightning and spontaneous combustion cause some fires, most are started by people.

Bush fires occur most frequently along the eastern coastal strip where serious fires occur on average once

*Australian Aboriginals used forest fires to flush out game. This hunting technique is common in Arnhem Land in the Northern Territory.*

every three years. In western Australia and southeastern Australia serious fires occur less often, about every ten to thirteen years.

In the summer of 1983, southern Australia was suffering from its third consecutive year of terrible drought. About 60 percent of the farming and grazing land was parched and useless. The weather was both dry and unbearably hot, with daytime temperatures soaring above 120 degrees Fahrenheit. The air and land were so dry that once fires started everything ignited instantly. High winds fanned the flames of the fires and pushed them rapidly across the hills. As the wind changed its course, both firefighters and people trying to escape the

*Airey's Inlet in Western Victoria, Australia, February 16, 1983. Bush-fires in the region were responsible for the ruins pictured here.*

flames were caught and killed. Witnesses reported that flames 100 feet high often advanced at more than a kilometer a minute, bursting into fireballs that roared like low-lying jets. The fire destroyed everything in its path. After the Australian Prime Minister, Malcolm Fraser, surveyed the damage, he said, "A Panzer [tank] division could not have caused so much damage. There is nothing left."

In parts of the western United States large forest fires similar to the Australian bush fires are a potential danger to communities in and near forested regions, especially after long summers with little or no rain. On Monday, November 24, 1980, such a fire erupted in the hills above San Bernardino, California. By Thanksgiving Day, November 27, 1980, the fire had raged for three and a half days and was still not under control. During that week 100 people had fled their mountain homes and gathered at an emergency evacuation church in the small town of Crestline. They had much for which to be thankful. All of them were safe, and although the terrible forest fire still raged in the hills nearby, most of their homes had been spared. Outside, the parking lot was loaded with cars that were stuffed with personal belongings and, in some cases, with house pets. For the past three days, they had lived in the buildings of the Thousand Pines Baptist Conference Center set up by the local Red Cross chapter as an evacuation camp. It would be several more days before the fire was under control and they would be able to return to their homes.

Many other people were not so lucky. In the northern San Bernardino suburbs, fierce winds—gusting at 90 miles per hour—had pushed the flames across the hills faster than firefighters could control them. Like a giant rolling furnace, the fire swept through neighborhoods. By the time the fire was finally out, 400 structures had burned, 284 families had lost their homes, and 4 people had died. More than 23,000 acres of brush land were destroyed with damage estimated at more than 40 million dollars.

Forest fires destroy thousands of acres of American wilderness every year. Some of these fires are started by lightning. However, about 80 percent are started by people, either by accident or on purpose. In either case, once the fire has begun, it rages through the forest in the same way, and the potential for destruction and loss of life is great.

In the fall of 1980 the weather in the San Bernardino

*Wind driven fires destroyed or damaged 240 homes in San Bernardino, California, November 1980.*

Mountains had been hot and dry. There had been no rain for months, and the grass and low shrubs on the base of the mountain were very dry. Experts determined that the San Bernardino fire was started by an arsonist in a canyon north of the city. Almost instantly, the fire grew to an inferno, racing over the hills and billowing black smoke into the sky.

As the fire swept south and westward, it consumed everything in its path. While they could, people attempted to save their homes by hosing down the roofs with water. But the fire was too hot and swift to be turned back, and people were forced to flee.

When people could take their pets or livestock with them, they did, but many animals were left on their own or brought to the city animal shelter. At the peak of the crisis the animal shelter resembled a crowded barnyard, housing about thirty horses, ponies, donkeys and mules, two bulls, five steers, ten goats, a cow, about two dozen hogs, a sow and her eight piglets, a ram and about fifty chickens and ducks. This was in addition to dozens of cats and dogs brought in for the emergency.

Within a few hours after the fire started, the residents of San Bernardino County began to make plans to help the people who had lost their homes. Local radio stations broadcast a plea from the San Bernardino mayor for the names of people who would be willing to share their homes and Thanksgiving dinner with the fire victims. The next day, the mayor's office was deluged with calls. There were offers of food, housing, clothing, baby food, and Thanksgiving dinner invitations. After more than 1,000 responses, the mayor's office was able to declare that it had met its goal, and no more donations were needed.

The Red Cross in San Bernardino received enormous piles of blankets and clothing for the fire victims, and aid poured in from other parts of the country as well. In one case, a woman in Memphis, Tennessee, whose uncle lived in San Bernardino, collected 130 boxes of clothing. These were then shipped, free of charge, by Federal Express. In communities nearby, high school students, 4-H Clubs, churches, and community groups collected

PROMOTION AUSTRALIA

*Fire victims receive clothes and bedding at Red Cross shelter, San Bernardino, California, November 1980.*

clothing and food. Local businesses helped by offering special credit terms to fire victims, and local restaurants fed or provided food for firefighters and fire victims. In many other cases, offers of help were personal—from one family to another and from one stranger to another.

*Volunteer helps fire victim understand how she can get disaster aid at a Red Cross service in San Bernardino, California, November, 1980.*

In the weeks that followed the fire disaster, many relief agencies worked to help the fire victims. Through the Red Cross, people received food, clothing, temporary housing, medical aid, household items, and temporary minor home repairs. Many people who had lost their homes were able to get money to rebuild through their insurance policies. Nearly 300 people sought help from the Federal Emergency Management Agency disaster assistance center located in the National Guard Armory in San Bernardino.

Even after the ashes had cooled and rebuilding began, danger caused by the fire remained. When the winter and spring rains came, the fire-scoured landscape would not be able to absorb the run-off, greatly increasing the likelihood of floods and mudslides. The only prevention was to replant quickly and to hope for light rains.

By early December, volunteers had started planting grass seed on the San Bernardino foothills. The Tree People, a Southern California environmental and reforestation organization, brought in volunteers to plant thousands of seedlings on the higher slopes. Replanting was also done by the United States Forest Service, which used helicopters to spread grass seed and fertilizer over 8,000 acres. Despite all these efforts, there was no guarantee that this would prevent flooding. Many San Bernardino residents placed sandbags around their homes as a precaution. Luckily, the rains that year were light, and there was no serious flooding.

Naturally started fires, usually ignited by lightning, have burned across the land for centuries and are part of the cycle of growth and replenishment of forests and grasslands. Fires are also sometimes started by *spontaneous combustion* or hot volcanic rock. By clearing forests of dead wood, diseased plants, and dense undergrowth, fires make room for healthy plants to grow stronger and for new plants to get a start. Many plants, including trees like the giant sequoia of the Sierra Nevada Mountains in California, need fires to reproduce. Their seed cones need the heat of the fire to open.

When naturally started fires occur on a regular cycle

they are low burning and limited in scope. However, when a forest has not burned for a long time, a great amount of debris accumulates on the forest floor, providing fuel for a terrible *conflagration*. Fires like these destroy everything, including the seeds for regrowth. Today, many of the national forests in the United States are overgrown due to a vigorous program of fire prevention during the first half of the century. The United States Forest Service is now clearing some of these forests, and when there is a small fire they often let it burn out as long as the flames are under control and do not endanger people or property.

Devastating fires are a threat throughout the forested areas of the world, destroying millions of acres of valuable timberland each year. In May 1987 a giant fire raged through northeastern China and was reported to be the worst that country had experienced in 40 years. At least 200 people were killed, two towns destroyed, and a year's supply of timber ruined in a country which already had a shortage of timber resources.

The fire in China apparently broke out on May 5 in the Gulian Forest, a restricted area in northern China adjacent to the Soviet border. A Chinese newspaper reported that the fire started when an oil leak from a bush-cutting machine ignited. As the fire took hold it swept through dense groups of pines. The pitch in the trees became a powerful fuel and the fire exploded into huge balls of flame. These rolling infernos sped through the air at nearly 70 miles an hour, so fast that unwary villagers became caught in their paths. The town of Tuqiang was wiped out in just 20 minutes on the evening of May 7. The fire came at such speed that most people were trapped in their homes with no chance of escape.

For more than two weeks 35,000 firefighters battled

to control the huge fire. Along the western edge of the fire they excavated a large U-shaped firebreak 180 miles long. Chemical extinguishers were also used to bring the fire under control. According to Chinese reports more than 800,000 acres of forest vanished and nearly 50 million dollars of property was destroyed.

Most forest fires occur in wilderness areas, but they are a danger to people who live in or at the edge of a forest, especially when weather conditions contribute to uncontrolled burning. The worst fire in the United States, in terms of lives lost, occurred in October 1871 in Peshtigo, Wisconsin, a small lumber town north of Green Bay. A *drought* had dried out the surrounding forest so thoroughly that it was impossible to keep fires from starting spontaneously in the smoldering peat bog that surrounded the town. Fires would travel slowly underground and then suddenly burst into flames on the surface. That fall, a cloud of smoke hung permanently over the town.

Then, on the night of October 8, 1871, a huge fire, fanned by hot winds, suddenly erupted. With ferocious speed it engulfed the town, killing two-thirds of its 2,000 inhabitants. The fire raged on, eventually destroying two more towns and over a million acres of timberland.

Although the Peshtigo fire was terrible, few know about it, because it occurred on the same day as the great Chicago fire that destroyed much of that city. The Governor of Wisconsin had to make a special appeal so that people would send disaster aid to the Peshtigo victims as well as to Chicago.

Today's fire fighters are much more highly trained than those who tried to battle the Peshtigo blaze. Intensive training, peak conditioning, up-to-date equipment, and dedication are characteristics of modern firefighting.

# CHAPTER NINE

# Preparing for Natural Disasters

The most violent earthquake in United States history was felt over an area of a million square miles, yet almost no lives were lost. It occurred on December 16, 1811 and was centered in the tiny town of New Madrid, Missouri. Although the series of giant tremors permanently altered the landscape—creating new lakes, shifting the course of rivers, and cracking open the earth in places—so few people lived in the area at the time that there were relatively few injuries. If such an earthquake occurred today, there would be widespread catastrophe. In the last 200 years the population of the world has increased dramatically and many more people live in areas prone to disaster from natural events.

The impact of a disaster on a community depends on when it occurs, the density of the population, the resources of the community, and how well the people are prepared. A disaster that occurs when most people are at home is likely to cause less disruption than one that occurs when people are at school or at work. For instance, if the San Fernando, California earthquake of 1971, a tremor which destroyed freeway overpasses and bridges, had occurred during rush hour instead of the early morning, a great many more people would have been injured.

*Mount St. Helens, Washington.*

*Mount Pelée, Martinique.*

When Mount St. Helens exploded in May 1980, the destruction was massive, but relatively few people lost their lives. Fortunately, the volcano was in a wilderness area that was largely uninhabited. Also, in anticipation of the eruption most people had been evacuated. On the other hand, the tragedy of the Mount Pelée eruption in Martinique in May 1902—where 40,000 people died— was that the people who lived in the bustling resort city at the base of the volcano had ignored warning signs and remained in the danger zone.

Natural disaster can occur anywhere. However, people in developed countries have a much better chance of coping with and recovering from disaster than people in underdeveloped or developing nations. For instance, in the United States, most people have insurance against natural disasters, and in addition to that, the government provides funds for disaster recovery. In countries like East Pakistan (Bangladesh), people have barely enough to live on, and they have no domestic resources to help them recover from disasters.

In 1970, when a terrible cyclone swept over Bangladesh, it literally washed away everything—people, animals, houses, and crops. Villagers described the flooding in one of two ways: either as a gradual wave rising from 8 to 20 feet over a period of hours, or as a thunderous roar followed by a massive wall of water. In both cases there were huge numbers of deaths, all within the brief period of a single night. Where the water rose gradually, people climbed to the roofs of their houses or climbed trees. However, the houses frequently collapsed, and the trees were difficult to hang onto in the face of 90-mile-per-hour winds. Where the waves struck suddenly people were simply washed away. When the water receded, those not washed out to sea were often found

*Bushfire catastrophe in February 1983. Burned out cars in Cockatoo, South Eastern Australia.*

miles inland or caught in the branches of a distant tree. So many people were missing that it was difficult to know exactly how many died. Government health officials estimated that more than a quarter of a million people were killed. For the survivors, it was only the beginning of their misery. Because of problems elsewhere, the government provided relief slowly and half-heartedly. By the time it came, many had already died of starvation, injury, and disease. The disruption and social disorder caused by the cyclone were factors in the rebellion against the government later on.

Although there is no way to prevent natural disasters from occurring, the best way to insure survival and a quick recovery is with adequate preparation. Many communities have plans for what to do in an emergency, with special duties for fire fighters, police, and medical personnel. Most schools and businesses also have plans for what to do in an emergency.

If your family is home, it is important to know where to find emergency supplies and what to do in an emergency. If a major disaster occurs, there may be no one available to help your family right away. Even if property is not damaged or no one is injured, it may be necessary to take care of yourselves for a while. Roads may be blocked, electricity and telephone lines may be down, or gas and water lines may be broken. It could be several days before services are restored.

Although each disaster creates its own special problems, all share some common elements. The following list of emergency supplies to be kept at home is recommended by the American Red Cross. These enable a family to live independently for 72 hours or more after a major disaster. A two-week supply is recommended as a minimum reserve of water, food, medicine, and other consumable items.

## *Home Emergency Supplies*

Survival

    Water—2 quarts to 1 gallon per person per day

    First Aid Kit—ample and freshly stocked

    First Aid Book—know how to use it

    Food—canned or individually packaged. Pre-cooked and/

or requiring minimum heat and water. Consider babies, pets, and other special food needed.

Can opener

Blankets—or sleeping bag for each member of family

Radio—portable battery-operated. Spare batteries.

Critical medication and glasses—if needed

Fire extinguisher

Flashlight—fresh and spare batteries and bulb

Watch or clock—battery or spring-wound

Sanitation Supplies

Large plastic trash bags—for trash, waste, water protection, ground cloth

Large trash cans

Hand soap

Liquid detergent

Shampoo

Toothpaste and toothbrush

Pre-moistened towelettes

Deodorant

Dentures

Feminine supplies

Infant supplies

Toilet paper

Powdered chlorinated lime—add to sewage to deodorize, disinfect and keep away insects.

Newspapers—to wrap garbage and waste. Can also be used for warmth.

Safety

Heavy shoes—for every family member

Heavy gloves—for every person clearing debris

Candles

Matches—dipped in wax and kept in waterproof container

Knife—sharp, or razor blades

Garden hose—for siphoning and fire fighting

Cooking

Barbeque—charcoal and lighter or Sterno stove (use outdoors only)

Plastic Bags—various sizes, sealable

Pots—at least two
Paper plates
Plastic knives, forks, spoons
Paper towels
Tools
  Axe
  Shovel
  Broom
  Crescent wrench—for turning off gas main
  Screwdriver
  Pliers
  Hammer
  Coil of ½-inch rope
  Coil of baling wire
  Plastic tape
  Pen and paper
Car Mini-Survival Kit
  Non-perishable food—store in empty coffee cans
  Bottled water
  First aid kit
  Flares
  Fire extinguisher
  Blanket
  Sealable plastic bags
  Flashlight—fresh and spare batteries and bulb
  Critical medication
  Tools—screwdriver, pliers, wire, knife
  Short rubber hose—for siphoning
  Small package of tissues
  Pre-moistened towelettes
  Sturdy shoes

Most of the items on the lists are usually available at home and can be assembled quickly. If your family must leave the house, remind your parents to leave a message telling people where you can be found. In addition to being generally prepared for emergencies, there are particular things to remember for each kind of natural disaster.

*Floods*

If you live in an area that is threatened by floods, the Red Cross makes the following recommendations. When rising water threatens your home, everything possible should be moved to the upper floors of the house or to another safe place on high ground. Then, if the water seems headed for your house or if the authorities order you to leave, your family should make arrangements to go to a designated safe place. If the water is rising rapidly, it is best to leave right away. Otherwise, before leaving, adult members of your household should disconnect electrical appliances and move small appliances and motors to upper floors. Remind your parents to turn off the main electrical switch and cover the electrical outlets before leaving. They should also take with them important papers, eyeglasses, prescription medicines, and other essential items.

When a flood is over, authorities will not allow your family to return home unless it is safe. Do not drink the water from a faucet unless it is determined to be safe. Officials of the county health department are responsible for testing water supplies and for advising people whether or not it is safe to use the water. If they determine that the water is contaminated, they prohibit its use until further notice. If your family is unsure about the safety of the water in your community after a disaster such as a flood, the best thing to do is to check with the local health department.

After your home has been flooded, you should not turn on any electrical appliances until they have been checked—wet wires are dangerous. If you smell escaping gas, urge your parents to report it immediately. Encourage and help your family throw out food that had spoiled in the freezer or refrigerator. Follow the guidance of authorities in cleaning up and resuming normal life.

## Earthquakes

If you live in a part of the world where earthquakes occur, homes in earthquake-prone areas should be checked for hazards such as heavy objects stored on high shelves. Family earthquake drills are also recommended. A plan for how a family will get back together if members are at school or at work is another important preparation measure. All adults in the family should know how to turn off gas, electricity, and water at the main valves.

When an earthquake occurs the most important thing to do is the hardest, and that is to stay calm.

The Red Cross makes the following recommendations for what to do during an actual earthquake. If you are indoors, stay there. Get under a sturdy table or desk or brace yourself in a doorway or corner. Move to an inside hallway when possible. Choose a location that will allow you air to breathe if the building collapses around you. Stay clear of windows, bookcases, china cabinets, heavy mirrors, hanging plants, and other objects. Watch out for falling plaster. If you are outside, move to an open area away from power lines and poles, trees, walls, and chimneys. In a crowded store or other public place, do not rush for exits. Move away from display shelves containing objects that may fall. In a high-rise building, get under a desk and stay away from windows. Stay in the building on the same floor. Avoid using the elevator because the power may go off. Don't be surprised if the fire alarm or sprinkler systems go on. If you are in a car, the driver should pull to the side of the road and stop the car. Everyone should stay in the car until the shaking

*Cracked road in San Fernando Valley, California, following earthquake of 1971.*

has stopped. After the earthquake is over, cars should not try to cross bridges or overpasses that may have been damaged.

After an earthquake, the first thing to do is to check for injuries and seek first aid if necessary. If you are at home, an adult should check to see if gas, water, or sewage lines have broken, and if any electrical lines are down. Utilities should be turned off if necessary, and building damage should be assessed. Shoes should always be worn to protect against broken glass. Instructions from the authorities will be given in radio broadcasts. Telephones should only be used in emergencies; lines need not be jammed with unnecessary calls.

## Avalanches

Today, as more and more people become involved in winter sports and venture into wilderness areas, it is important to learn to recognize the danger signs of a possible avalanche. Avalanche experts advise people to avoid slopes where chutes are loaded with wind-blown snow and to stay on the windward side of a slope. Skiers should also avoid terrain where, if they get caught, they can be carried over a cliff, buried in a deep gully, or swept into water. The danger from avalanches can be minimized as long as people respect their potential power.

## Blizzards

During the winter, families should be able to live independently for a short time if electricity or fuel supply is cut off, or if roads are blocked by a storm. Battery-powered equipment, extra food, and other emergency supplies should be set aside. When outdoors, dressing with several layers of protective clothing is more effective than with single layers of thick clothing.

Mittens are better than gloves. Hoods or scarves can be used to cover the mouth and protect the lungs from extremely cold air.

People who drive in winter need to be extra careful, and it is important to keep a car "winterized" so that it will start in cold weather. Talk to your parents about keeping a winter emergency kit in the family car. It should contain equipment to keep you warm, visible, and alive if you are trapped on the road in a winter storm. Specific items to include are a first-aid kit, wool blankets, high energy food such as candy, dried fruit, or unsalted nuts, flares, and a flashlight.

If trapped by a blizzard, avoid getting wet and cold, stay in your car, keep it ventilated, and turn on the inside light at night. If a large snowstorm is predicted, the best thing to do is to stay home until it is over, and wait until the roads are clear before going out.

*Tornadoes*

If caught in a tornado's path, the safest place to be is the basement of a building or in a "storm cellar," an underground room constructed specially as a tornado shelter. If there is no time to go to a shelter, the best thing to do is to get under a sturdy table or other heavy piece of furniture that protects from glass and flying debris. If caught outside and there is a tornado, people are advised to lie down in a ditch or a deep hollow.

One of the best ways adults learn what to do in the event of a disaster is by taking classes in first aid and disaster training. In many cases, such classes are offered at community centers, Red Cross offices, schools, businesses, hospitals. Children obtain emergency training through groups such as Girl Scouts or Boy Scouts. If you and your family know what to do, and what *not* to do, in an emergency, you are much less likely to panic and will be able to provide useful assistance.

All kinds of disasters, both natural and man-made, happen every day. If we are lucky, most of us will never have to face a major disaster personally. Yet, it is always reassuring to know that if there is an emergency, there are many people we can depend on to help.

# Glossary

*after shock*—a secondary earth tremor following an earthquake

*Agency for International Development* (AID)—U.S. government agency which provides loans and grants to underdeveloped countries

*ARC*—American Red Cross

*atom bomb*—a bomb whose explosive force comes from a chain reaction based on the nuclear fission of uranium or plutonium

*avalanche*—a mass of snow, ice, or stones rapidly falling down the side of a mountain

*bush fires*—Australian term for forest fires

*CARE*—Cooperative for American Relief to Everywhere

*Caritas Internationalis*—International Confederation of Catholic Organizations for Charitable and Social Action

*conflagration*—a large destructive fire

*continental plate*—large section of the earth's crust

*CRS*—Catholic Relief Services

*CWS*—Church World Service, a division of Overseas Ministries of the National Council of Churches in the U.S.

*cyclone*—a large circular storm originating over warm tropical waters

*Disaster Relief Act,* 1970—a U.S. government program designed to provide financial aid and low-interest loans to disaster victims

*earthquake*—an underground shock that makes part of the earth's surface tremble

*ecology*—the relationship of plants and animals to their environment *emergency phase*—the first few hours and days following a disaster during which people need food, temporary shelter, and urgent medical care

*erdalator*—a large water purification device

*Flood Disaster Protection Act,* 1973—an extension of the Disaster Relief Act to provide aid to victims of floods and tornadoes

*fjord*—a long narrow arm of the sea bordered by steep cliffs

*flood plain*—a nearly flat plain along the course of a stream or river that is naturally subject to flooding at high water

*flood walls*—barriers built at the edges of the sea to prevent flooding by large waves

*flood ways*—pathways built to help flood waters bypass populated areas

*forest fire*—the uncontrolled burning of forest or shrub land

*hurricane*—see cyclone

*ICRC*—International Committee of the Red Cross

*ITU*—International Telecommunications Union

*Krakatoa*—volcanic island in Indonesia which violently erupted in 1883

*levee*—a bank built to keep a river from overflowing

*LWF*—Lutheran World Federation

*Lutheran World Relief*—a subcommittee of LWF

*MEDICO*—Medical International Cooperation Organization, a service of CARE

*NEC*—National Emergency Committee

*non-partisan*—not affiliated with nor adherent to a party, faction, cause, person or government

*OXFAM*—Oxford Committee for Famine Relief

*plate techtonics*—the study of how the earth's continental plates move

*Richter scale*—a scale which uses mathematical formulas to measure the amount of energy generated by an earthquake

*reconstruction period*—the weeks and months following a disaster during which disaster victims are cleaning up and rebuilding their community

*rift*—the gap formed when one of the earth's continental plates cracks and the two pieces move apart

*Ring of Fire*—the circle of volcanoes bordering the Pacific Ocean

*Save the Children*—an international relief organization

*short-wave radios*—high frequency radio waves used to communicate over short distances (as in citizen's band radios). They can also be used over long distances.

*seismology*—the science or study of earthquakes and their phenomena

*spontaneous combustion*—the process of catching fire due to heat generated by internal chemical processes

*Steering Committee*—coordinating committee for disaster relief of OXFAM, CRS, WCC, LWF, and the League of Red Cross Societies

*tidal wave*—high ocean wave caused by the gravitational pull of the moon

*tornado*—a destructive funnel-shaped windstorm

*tremor*—the shaking of the earth as caused by an earthquake

*tsunami*—an extremely long and low sea wave generated by an earthquake, landslide, volcano, or explosion

*typhoon*—see cyclone

*UNDRO*—Office of the United Nations Disaster Relief

*UNICEF*—United Nations International Childrens' Fund

*United Way*—centralized fundraising organization for a variety of charitable, nonprofit groups

*volcanic eruption*—the explosive emission of smoke, lava, or ashes from a volcano

*volcano*—a mountain with an opening in its top leading to molten rock beneath the earth's crust

*Weather Watch*—a program that is part of WMO, which provides warning of disasters such as hurricanes

*WCC*—World Council of Churches

*WFP*—World Food Program

*WHO*—World Health Organization

*WMO*—World Meteorological Organization

# Suggestions for Further Reading

Isaac Asimov, HOW DID WE FIND OUT ABOUT VOLCA-
NOES? (Walker, 1981).

Thomas Aylesworth, GEOLOGICAL DISASTERS: EARTH-
QUAKES AND VOLCANOES, (Watts, 1979).

Melvin Berger, DISASTROUS FLOODS AND TIDAL
WAVES and DISASTROUS VOLCANOES, (Watts, 1981).

Elizabeth Clemons, WAVES, TIDES AND CURRENTS, (Alfred A. Knopf, 1967).

Cricket Magazine, June 1987.

Marshall Fishwick, CLARA BARTON, (Silver Burdett, 1966).

Ronald Fodor, EARTH AFIRE! VOLCANOES AND THEIR
ACTIVITY, (Morrow, 1981).

Dennis B. Fradin, DISASTER! EARTHQUAKES, DISASTER!
FLOODS, DISASTER! TORNADOES, and DISASTER!
VOLCANOES, (Children's Press, 1982); DISASTER! BLIZ-
ZARDS AND WINTER WEATHER and DISASTER!
DROUGHTS, (Children's Press, 1983).

Henry Gilfond, DISASTROUS EARTHQUAKES, (Watts,
1981).

Anthony Greenbank, A HANDBOOK FOR EMERGEN-
CIES: COMING OUT ALIVE, (Doubleday, 1975, 1976).

Gary Jennings, KILLER STORMS: HURRICANES, TY-
PHOONS AND TORNADOES, (Harper and Row, 1970).

Virginia Kimball, EARTHQUAKE READY, (Peace Press,
1981).

Patricia Lauber, VOLCANO: THE ERUPTION AND HEAL-

ING OF MOUNT ST. HELENS, (Lothrop, Lee & Shepard, 1986).

George Laycock, TORNADOES, KILLER STORMS, (David McKay, 1979).

Hershell Nixon and Joan Nixon, EARTHQUAKES, NATURE IN MOTION, (Dodd, 1981).

Marian Place, MOUNT ST. HELENS: A SLEEPING VOLCANO AWAKES, (Dodd, 1978).

Seymour Simon, DANGER FROM BELOW: EARTHQUAKES PAST, PRESENT AND FUTURE, (Four Winds, 1979).

Harold and Geraldine Woods, THE UNITED NATIONS, (Watts, 1985).

# Selected Bibliography

Lincoln C. Chen, Ed., DISASTER IN BANGLADESH: HEALTH CRISES IN A DEVELOPING NATION, (Oxford University Press, 1973).

James Cornell, THE GREAT INTERNATIONAL DISASTER BOOK, (Scribners, 1976).

DISASTER RELIEF: Case Report, Guatemala Earthquake, February 1976, (Agency for International Development, 1978).

Elizabeth A. Fisher and Robert A. Hadley, "Two Ancient Accounts of the Eruption of Mount Vesuvius in A.D. 79," POMPEII AND THE VESUVIAN LANDSCAPE, (Smithsonian Institution, 1979).

Stephen Green, INTERNATIONAL DISASTER RELIEF, (McGraw-Hill, 1977).

A GUIDE TO FOOD AND HEALTH RELIEF OPERATIONS FOR DISASTERS, (United Nations, 1977).

E. Roland Harriman, AGNES, (American Red Cross, 1972).

Frances Kennett, THE GREATEST DISASTERS OF THE TWENTIETH CENTURY, (Marshall Cavendish Publications, 1975).

NATIONAL GEOGRAPHIC MAGAZINE, March 1975, June 1976, June 1987, September 1980, September 1982, May 1986.

SAFETY AND SURVIVAL IN AN EARTHQUAKE, (American Red Cross, 1982).

Bruce Tegner and Alice McGrath, THE SURVIVAL BOOK, (Bantam Books, 1982).

# Index